Prayer

Prayer

THE CRY FOR THE KINGDOM

REVISED EDITION

Stanley J. Grenz

William B. Eerdmans Publishing Company
Grand Rapids, Michigan / Cambridge, U.K.

To my mother,

in gratitude for her prayers

First edition © 1988 Hendrickson Publishers, Inc.
Revised edition © 2005 Wm. B. Eerdmans Publishing Co.
All rights reserved

Wm. B. Eerdmans Publishing Co.
255 Jefferson Ave. S.E., Grand Rapids, Michigan 49503 /
P.O. Box 163, Cambridge CB3 9PU U.K.
www.eerdmans.com

Printed in the United States of America

09 08 07 06 05   7 6 5 4 3 2

Library of Congress Cataloging-in-Publication Data

Grenz, Stanley J. (Stanley James), 1950-2005.
    Prayer: the cry for the kingdom / Stanley J. Grenz. — Rev. ed.
        p.   cm.
    Includes bibliographical references (p.   ).
    ISBN 0-8028-2847-7 (pbk.: alk. paper)
        1. Prayer. I. Title.

  BV210.3.G736   2005
  248.3'2 — dc22

                        2005040494

Unless otherwise noted, Scripture references are taken from two sources:
• THE HOLY BIBLE: NEW INTERNATIONAL VERSION. Copyright © 1973, 1978, 1984 by
  the International Bible Society. Used by permission of Zondervan Bible Publishers.
• THE HOLY BIBLE: NEW INTERNATIONAL VERSION, INCLUSIVE LANGUAGE
  EDITION. Copyright © 1995, 1996 by Hodder & Stoughton.

Contents

Foreword, *by Eugene Peterson*   vii

Preface   ix

PROLOGUE: A Call to Prayer   1

1. The Nature of Christian Prayer   8
   The Background to the Christian Concept of Prayer   9
   Prayer and the Life of Jesus   14
   Prayer in the New Testament Church   23
   Christian Prayer and the Church of All Ages   26

2. How Petitionary Prayer "Works"   31
   What Supplication "Effects"   32
   Prayer and Modern Psychology   36
   Prayer and Christian Theology   43

3. What Praying according to God's Will Means   54
   The Characteristics of the Petitioner   55
   The Characteristics of the Petition   63

4. How to Pray according to God's Will   67
   The General Pattern   67
   Praying in Situations of Christian Concern   69

Praying for the Sick   *84*

Praying Specifically   *90*

5. Persisting in Prayer   93

   Jesus' Command to Persistency   *94*

   The Importance of Persistency   *99*

   The Persistent Attitude   *102*

6. Practicing Effective Prayer   105

   Praying in Public Worship   *107*

   Praying Alone   *111*

   Praying Together   *116*

   EPILOGUE: The Life of Prayer   122

   Selected Bibliography   125

Foreword

A shift took place in Western society and culture about three to four hundred years ago that radically disrupted our continuity with earlier civilizations. For convenience (sacrificing accuracy), the shift has been labeled The Age of Enlightenment. The shift was seismic: men and women took over and occupied center stage, displacing God and gods. The assumptions of millennia — that God (or gods) defined and accounted for the world and everything in it — were discarded and replaced with the conviction that the human person was perfectly capable of running things on his or her own. Rapid developments in exploration and invention, learning and technology, offered confirmation that we humans on our own could do pretty much anything we wanted to do. If we were not yet in total control, it looked very much as if it wouldn't be long before we were.

It is not that God (for biblical people) and gods (for the others) were no longer present; it is simply that they were pushed to the margins, off in the wings, offstage or backstage. The consequences of that shift from God at the center to men and women at the center is that, unlike most of our ancestors, whether biblical or pagan, we no longer live in a praying world. We have grown up in a world in which the primary way in which language is used is by men and women talking to and listening to one another, not listening to and answering God.

For prayer means dealing personally and seriously with God as the central reality of life. If God is no longer central, dominating all that is, was, and will be, prayer atrophies into an occasional and spasmodic ceremonial verbal gesture or a desperate lunge for miracle, neither of which has any support in everyday life.

Meanwhile, Christians pray. But if we are to continue to pray out of the center of our lives, and not just timidly or occasionally from the margins, we need to take deliberate measures to counter the dismissal and trivialization of prayer that characterize our culture — satirized by one of our poets (John Fowles) as "trying to carry water in a leaky bucket." This book is such a measure, a deliberate counter to the assumptions of our culture that life is all about us, all about what we can do. It is a deliberate counter to the assumption that language is primarily designed for communication with one another, telling one another what we know and feel and want from life and replacing that assumption with the conviction that our language originates in God revealing himself to us and then as a gift to us to respond to God. Stanley Grenz provides us with witness and witnesses to the primacy and centrality of prayer — witness and witnesses that put us back in the robust company of our biblical ancestors. We recover our sense of God-centrality and its corollary, prayer-reality. The witness and witnesses return us to our praying lives with a renewed sense of being in on the main action.

Dr. Grenz's sudden and untimely death in the spring of 2005 is a keenly felt loss in the Christian community. But his many books continue to keep his voice alive among us. The subtitle of this book, *The Cry for the Kingdom,* is a fitting epitaph to his life, reverberating both through these pages and through our lives, an antidote first to the anemia and then to the triviality that the non-praying world assigns to prayer. The first word conveys urgency: *Cry* — prayer is not a leisure-time activity. Matters of life and death, salvation and judgment, suffering and justice, peace and war, recrimination and reconciliation are being worked out in our families and among our neighbors all the time, in our nation and the world all the time. We must not be silent and passive spectators to any of it. We find ourselves, quite miraculously, on the front lines, where God's praying people have always found themselves.

The last word places our prayers in the largest imaginable context: *Kingdom* — the comprehensive sovereignty of "God my king . . . , working salvation in the midst of the earth" (Ps. 74:12). There is a lot going on all around us, with very little of the real action reported by newspaper and television. Our prayers wake us up to what is going on, first to the immensity of it all and then to the minute particulars. Our prayers wake us up to what God is doing all the time and everywhere. And then they make us participants from right where we are.

Yes, *Cry for the Kingdom,* by all means.

EUGENE H. PETERSON
Professor Emeritus of Spiritual Theology, Regent College, Vancouver

Preface

I was raised in a home and a church community in which prayer was assumed to be an integral part of the "normal" Christian life. From an early age, I was led to believe that everyone — at least everyone I knew — prayed regularly and fervently. Moreover, everyone I knew believed that their prayers actually made a difference in this world.

In our family, "normal" praying included saying "grace" before meals. This was to be done not only when we were at home or at church potlucks, but also when we ate out — whether in the car at a drive-in or even in a restaurant. So ingrained in my psyche was the importance of this practice that I would automatically wait for my host to pray whenever I sat down to a meal at a friend's house. After supper — before we "kids" were allowed to leave the table to do the evening dishwashing chore, to play with our friends, or to get started on our schoolwork — we would invariably have "family devotions." This nightly routine included reading a passage from the Bible, together with the corresponding piece from the devotional booklet "Our Daily Bread," and then sharing a time of prayer. The tasks of reading and praying were not fulfilled by our parents alone. As soon as the three of us children were able to read or pray, we too were added to the rotation.

The churches that my father, the Reverend Richard A. Grenz, served as pastor were filled with people who prayed just as we did. Or at least they were supposed to, if they were "normal" Christians. Prayer was likewise viewed as part of "normal" congregational life. Sunday-morning worship services always included a slot for the "pastoral prayer." Sunday-evening gatherings would often include opportunities for several people in the congregation to pray publicly. And all such prayers, like the "pasto-

ral prayer" that my father offered Sunday mornings, were extemporaneous. The weekly church calender also included the Wednesday (or Thurs-
day) evening "Hour of Power," which was divided between a Bible study
and a time of prayer. During the latter, those in attendance would sepa-
rate into men's and women's groups. "Men" included any male children
present. And "cottage" prayer meetings in preparation for the annual
evangelistic and "deeper life" meetings were also staples of congregational life. Although as a child I didn't relish being required to attend
these various prayer gatherings, as an adult I came to realize how much
they had shaped my understanding of what it means to participate in a
praying community and what seasoned, mature praying involves.

The tone for the "normal" prayer life that characterized both the
home and the churches in which I was raised was set by my father, who
was truly a man of prayer. I heard my father pray with his family and
with his church people, of course. But I also recall waking in what to me
seemed like the middle of the night and overhearing him praying with
my mother. And I remember as well catching glimpses of him kneeling
in the privacy of his study at church engaging in earnest prayer. When I
inherited his pastoral library upon his death at the age of fifty-six (when
I was twenty-one), I found two short books devoted to the practicalities
of following a forty-day period of fasting and prayer after the pattern of
Jesus himself. Although he never spoke much about his experiences in
following this discipline, I know that my father practiced fasting.

I must admit that I have never attained the level of devotion to
prayer that characterized my father's spiritual journey. Nevertheless,
prayer took on a heightened importance in my life when, in January
1979, after having completed graduate school, I became the pastor of a
bilingual (German-English) congregation in Winnipeg, Manitoba.
The Rowandale Baptist Church had been founded by immigrants
from the eastern provinces of Germany who had been displaced by the
advancing Soviet armies in the closing months of the Second World
War. During the two and a half years that I served as their pastor, I
found myself following many of the very practices that I had seen my
father fulfill during my childhood and teenage years. In Winnipeg I
also had occasion to attend two "Change the World School of Prayer"
seminars, sponsored by an organization that at that time was called
the World Literature Crusade. I, in turn, offered a series of Wednesay-
evening Bible studies that focused on the discipline of prayer.

In 1981 I left the pastorate to teach theology at the North American Baptist Seminary in Sioux Falls, South Dakota. A couple of years later, I sensed that I should offer a course for seminarians on the theology and practice of prayer. I determined that the focus of this course should not be the discipline of contemplative prayer, which at that time was already becoming increasingly popular. Rather, my intent was to engage with the petitionary aspect of prayer. I wanted to understand petitionary prayer theologically. My assumption was that a better theological understanding could facilitate more concerted — and as a consequence perhaps even more "effective" — praying. To prepare for the course, I read through nearly every book on the topic that I found on the shelves of the seminary library. However, my cursory reading did not lead me to a volume that I thought could serve as a core text for the proposed course. It was at that point that I decided to attempt to write a manuscript myself.

The response to the course emboldened me to look into the possibility of publishing the text. To this end, I sent query letters and copies of the manuscript to every publisher that would give me the time of day. Alas, no one on my list was willing to take a risk on the work of a young, unknown, and hitherto largely unpublished theologian — no one, that is, until a new start-up publishing house, Hendrickson Publishers, came on the scene. In 1988, my manuscript saw the light of day. Although it was the third volume that I had seen into print, it was the first that I had written solely on my own initiative and hence the first to give expression to a central passion of my own life and ministry.

After the book had enjoyed a happy fifteen-year run as a staple of the Hendrickson catalogue, the folks at the press informed me in July 2003 that they had sold the last copy and that *Prayer: The Cry for the Kingdom* was now out of print. One month later, the work had found a new home at the William B. Eerdmans Publishing Company. I found the enthusiasm of my friends at Eerdmans about the prospect of producing a second edition of the book gratifying and encouraging. The anticipation of publishing a new edition gave me the opportunity to thoroughly revise the book. This task included updating the language, rearranging several of the sections, and adding some newer materials. At the same time, I sought to maintain the integrity of the original composition, including leaving intact the central themes that I had spelled out nearly twenty years ago. The result is a revised edition in the true sense of the word, yet a revised edition of a volume that was composed at an earlier stage in my life.

I am grateful to the folks at Eerdmans for their willingness to bring this book back into print in its revised form. Although many people have been involved in the process, I would single out three: Michael Thomson, who so quickly expedited the idea of a second edition as an Eerdmans title; Sam Eerdmans, who expressed immediate enthusiasm for the project; and Mary Hietbrink, who ably guided *Prayer: The Cry for the Kingdom* through the publication process. I am also deeply honored that Eugene Peterson, my former colleague at Regent College in Vancouver, British Columbia, would take time from his busy schedule to introduce the book by means of a foreword.

Upon my father's death in 1971, my mother took over the role that my father bequeathed to her of being the chief pray-er in our family. Over thirty-three years later, she intercedes regularly not only for her three children, but also for their spouses, her five grandchildren, and her three great-grandchildren, in addition to the friends, neighbors, and other family members who populate her prayer list. I have personally sensed the depth of her prayer support for my ministry over the past decades. When *Prayer: The Cry for the Kingdom* was initially published, I dedicated the book to her. Rather than diminishing over the intervening years, her commitment to upholding her family, her church, and her world in prayer has intensified. Therefore, with an even deeper sense of gratitude, I gladly reaffirm the dedication of the revised edition to my praying mother, Clara Grenz.

STANLEY J. GRENZ
Christmas 2004

Prologue: A Call to Prayer

The church of Jesus Christ faces many challenges today. Yet the greatest challenge is not what might initially come to mind. The greatest challenge is not that of urging Christians to speak out on the great social issues of the day or to engage in political action, even though such involvements are crucial. Nor is our greatest challenge that of encouraging each other to be more fervent in evangelizing the world, even though evangelization ought to be of concern to every Christian. Rather, the greatest challenge facing the church of Jesus Christ today, and therefore every local congregation, is motivating the people of God to engage in sincere, honest, fervent prayer.

I believe that four considerations lead inevitably to this conclusion.

First, my contention that prayer is the greatest challenge to the church today is based on the experience of the early church as evidenced in the New Testament. The first-century community is a model of a praying church. The book of Acts presents the early Christians as a praying people. Already in the days prior to Pentecost, the Lord's disciples were devoted to prayer. Luke describes the upper-room experience as marked by continual prayer. In obedience to the command of Jesus (Acts 1:8), "they all joined together constantly in prayer" (Acts 1:14). Subsequent to Pentecost, the infant church in Jerusalem continued to be a praying community:

They devoted themselves to the apostles' teaching and to the fellowship, to the breaking of bread and to prayer.... Every day they continued to meet together in the temple courts. They broke bread in their

> homes and ate together with glad and sincere hearts, praising
> God. . . . (Acts 2:42, 46-47)

As a consequence, the Lord added "to their number daily those who
were being saved" (Acts 2:47).

Not only was the routine life of the early church marked by prayer,
but as a matter of course the believers turned to prayer in times of cri-
sis. For example, when the followers of Jesus heard the report of how
the authorities had commanded Peter and John not to preach in his
name, their immediate response was to take this difficulty to the Lord:
"They raised their voices together in prayer" (Acts 4:24). Later, when
King Herod arrested some of the members of the church, put James to
death, and then imprisoned Peter pending public trial (Acts 12:1-3), the
church prayed earnestly to God on his behalf. Even though they were
separated physically from their leader, the Christians rallied to his
cause by interceding for him.

The devotion to prayer that characterized the early community was
modeled by its leaders. For example, Peter's custom was to pause for
prayer at noon each day (Acts 10:9). Similarly, Paul's commitment to
prayer is evidenced by the great prayers that he included in his epistles
and by incidents in his life in which he naturally turned to prayer. During their sojourn in the city of Philippi, to cite one occasion, missionaries Paul and Silas were jailed, beaten, and put in stocks. Yet despite the
deep pain that they were suffering, they prayed and sung hymns of
praise to God well into the night (Acts 16:25).

The New Testament indicates that the devotion of the early believers to prayer was a key to their success. In fact, the Apostle Paul repeatedly reminded the readers of his epistles of the need for Christian intercession for the sake of the missionary enterprise. In one letter, he
declared forthrightly, "Devote yourselves to prayer, being watchful and
thankful. And pray for us, too, that God may open a door for our message, so that we may proclaim the mystery of Christ, for which I am in
chains. Pray that I may proclaim it clearly, as I should" (Col. 4:2-4).

The book of Acts also emphasizes the role of prayer in the success
of the early church. The empowerment by the Spirit of God on Pentecost was predicated by the prayer of the upper-room disciples (Acts
2:1-4). Later, the Spirit's filling them for the task of bold proclamation in the face of adversity came in response to prayer (4:31-33). Be-

cause they prayed, God intervened in times of danger (e.g., Acts 12:6-17; 16:26-31).

Moreover, prayer opened the way for great advances for the gospel. Cornelius, the first Gentile convert, heard the gospel because Peter was a man of prayer. In fact, it was during his time of daily prayer that the apostle received the vision from God that prompted him to respond positively to the request of Cornelius's emissaries to accompany them to his home. In a similar way, the sending of Paul as a missionary from Antioch was an outworking of the prayer life of that church. It was while they were "worshiping the Lord and fasting" that the Spirit commanded the church in Antioch to "set apart . . . Barnabas and Saul" (Acts 13:1-3).

Second, my claim that prayer is our greatest challenge arises from an honest appraisal of the state of the church today. If we look closely at the contemporary situation, we would likely find ourselves readily admitting that ours is the epitome of a prayerless church. This fact has been noted by many church leaders over the last several decades. In the late 1970s, for example, a prayer-movement leader observed,

> Not long ago a major denomination released a list of its top 12 priorities for their organization. Better Christian education was on the list as was improved pastoral counseling. Also mentioned was the goal of developing stronger youth and music programs for their churches. Local evangelism was given high priority. Unfortunately prayer wasn't even on the list.[1]

To be convinced of the basic truth of this observation, we need only ask ourselves, When was the last time that prayer was given top priority at any denominationally sponsored meeting or in any denominational promotion? Denominational programs readily target a variety of urgent tasks. Alas, prayer is rarely among them.

What is true on the denominational level is likewise present in many local churches: prayer receives little emphasis today. In most congregations, only a very small percentage of the worship service is devoted to prayer. Nor is prayer afforded a prominent place on the church

---

1. *Change the World School of Prayer Manual,* 2d ed., supplementary syllabus (Studio City, Calif.: World Literature Crusade, 1978), p. 2.

calendar. Prayer is a relatively insignificant aspect of the structured life of the people of God. Even the once traditional Wednesday-night prayer meeting (where it has survived) is no longer devoted to prayer but has become a "Bible study." This subtle change speaks volumes regarding the place of prayer in the life of the contemporary church.

Not only does prayer find little place in the structure of church life, but meager attention is devoted to fostering a praying congregation. For example, little emphasis is given in most churches to the task of developing praying, caring cell groups. Where small groups are encouraged, they all too often center on fellowship to the exclusion of prayer. Few congregations devote more than a bare minimum of time and resources to the task of teaching the people of God how to pray.

When it comes to prayer, denominations and churches are simply reflecting what is true of individual Christians. For many believers, prayer is a lost art. Many do not know how to pray and do not pray. For many of us, prayer is a source of guilt. The mere mention of the word results in an immediate recognition of our personal failure to pray as we should. Rather than being the source of feelings of joy and victory that it is intended to be, for most of us prayer triggers a sense of guilt and defeat!

Third, I believe that when we remind ourselves of the close relationship between prayer and renewal, we are driven to the conclusion that the greatest challenge facing the church today is that of motivating people to pray. Throughout church history an awakening to prayer among the people of God has constituted the key to church renewal. As one prayer leader aptly summarized the situation,

> Every spiritual awakening of significance from the beginning of Acts to the powerful Welsh revival early in this century had its roots in prayer. The awakenings under John Wesley, Jonathan Edwards and Charles Finney were first of all revivals of prayer. These religious leaders openly declared that prayer was the basis for all that happened in these world changing revivals.[2]

The awakening in America in 1857 provides an illuminating example. The glorious revival began when a humble lay worker in New York

---

2. *Change the World School of Prayer Manual*, p. 2. See also R. A. Torrey, *The Power of Prayer* (Grand Rapids: Zondervan, 1955), pp. 53-55, 242-45.

City, Jeremiah Lanphier, became burdened for what he saw as the lack of spiritual concern in the church. With another member of his congregation, Lanphier began a noon prayer meeting. Although few attended at first, God honored their efforts. Before long, as many as three thousand people came to the meetings. Eventually other prayer groups sprang up, with participants numbering in the tens of thousands. The result was a great revival that swept across the United States, in which hundreds of thousands accepted Jesus Christ as Savior.[3] Some suggest that it was this revival that saved the nation during turbulent times. Reflecting on the event from a vantage point nearly a century later, R. A. Torrey offered this opinion: "The whole emphasis was on prayer, and this whole nation was shaken by the power of God as it had never been shaken before, and perhaps has never been shaken since."[4]

A profound yet simple spiritual principle lies at the basis of the relationship between renewal and prayer that has been evident throughout history. Moral revival in a nation begins with the willingness of God's people to seek God's face in prayer.[5] God is the author of renewal, but in this task God wills the cooperation of human instruments. And at the heart of this cooperation is prayer. E. M. Bounds puts his finger on a principle that many Christian leaders have observed:

> All revivals are dependent upon God, but in revivals, as in other things, He invites and requires the assistance of man, and the full result is obtained when there is co-operation between the divine and the human. In other words, to employ a familiar phrase, God alone can save the world, but God cannot save the world alone. . . . "Revivals," as Dr. J. Wilbur Chapman reminds us, "are born in prayer."[6]

Finally, my claim that the greatest challenge facing the church is motivating the people of God to pray is an outworking of a truth regarding the relationship between prayer and the Christian. Prayer is perhaps the only task of the church in which everyone can participate. A person does not need special status, financial resources, or flashy

---

3. See Basil Miller, *Prayer Meetings That Made History* (Anderson, Ind.: Warner Press, 1938), pp. 51-56.

4. Torrey, *The Power of Prayer*, pp. 54-55.

5. See 2 Chronicles 7:14 for an Old Testament precedent of this principle.

6. Bounds, *Purpose in Prayer* (London: Marshall Brothers, n.d.), pp. 117-18.

spiritual gifts to be involved in this endeavor. On the contrary, any Christian — including the simplest and seemingly most insignificant saint — can become a giant of prayer. And through prayer, each Christian can play a crucial, vital role in renewal. In fact, any Christian can be the catalyst. Revival need not begin with the pastor, the deacons, the officers, or the prominent people of the church.

During one of Gypsy Smith's revival meetings, a pastor entreated the famous evangelist to pass on to him the secret of his success. "I want to know the best method of starting a spiritual awakening in my congregation," the pastor explained. To this query, Smith responded,

> Brother, go home and lock yourself in your room. Take a piece of chalk and draw a circle on the floor. Then get down on your knees inside that circle and confess all known sin. Determine to follow the Lord wherever His Word directs you, no matter what the cost. Ask Him to begin His work in you! When this prayer is answered, you will have the beginning of a revival in your church.

As this incident indicates, revival can begin with just one individual — indeed, with *any* individual — in the church.

The challenge of prayer, therefore, is not merely directed to the church as a whole. It comes to each Christian personally. S. D. Gordon articulated this well: "The greatest thing any one can do for God and for man is to pray. It is not the only thing. But it is the chief thing."[7] When believers dedicate themselves first individually and then corporately to the task of learning to pray, the Lord can and will use them to change the world.

But if prayer is the greatest challenge to the church, then why should we expend energy studying prayer? Prayer, it would seem, is not a topic to be discussed but a task to be done. Although this objection has some merit, it fails to take one important point into consideration. The actual situation regarding prayer is not so straightforward. Prayer is not something that we just do; it is a learned activity. Indeed, the disciples themselves requested of the Lord, "Teach us to pray" (Luke 11:1). And in response Jesus gave them what we know as the Lord's Prayer.

Prayer is learned by doing, of course. Yet praying well requires that

7. Gordon, *Quiet Talks on Prayer* (London: Revell, n.d.), p. 12.

we be taught to pray. At the heart of this "prayer training" is reflection, which includes the attempt to understand how prayer "works." Reflection on the working of prayer provides us with insight into the nature of prayer. As we come to understand more fully what prayer is and how prayer brings its divinely intended results, we are assisted in the task of eliminating the intellectual and volitional roadblocks to the life of prayer.

The importance of learning to pray is underscored by another consideration as well. For many people, prayer seems to be almost second nature. Yet the ability to pray well is not ingrained in us. Rather, it is learned. To state the point in another manner, anyone can "say a prayer," but true praying is a learned art that is developed in part through a growing understanding of how prayer functions. In this sense, prayer is analogous to human communication. The desire to communicate with others is a natural human drive. Yet as we repeatedly experience in our lives and in our relationships with others, the ability to communicate well is rare. All people communicate, but few are good communicators. So also with prayer: Many people pray, but true communication with God is learned. It is the result of both intellectual reflection and personal diligence.

Therefore, we must not only pray. We must also reflect on the nature and the working of prayer. As we do so, we discover that ultimately all prayer is a cry for the kingdom. When we come to comprehend this basic truth regarding prayer, we are better equipped to become effective pray-ers for the sake of the kingdom of God.

1. The Nature of Christian Prayer

In his *Letters and Papers from Prison,* the famous German theologian Dietrich Bonhoeffer recounts an incident that he experienced while he was incarcerated in a Nazi concentration camp. During one particularly heavy bombing raid, one of the prisoners who was normally quite frivolous lay on the floor moaning, "O God, O God." Bonhoeffer reports that he could not bring himself to offer the man "any Christian encouragement or comfort." He could not do so in part because he simply was not convinced that the man was in fact voicing a petition.[1]

As this incident suggests, at some elementary level prayer seems to be a common human response. In times of trial, people almost automatically find themselves moaning "O God!"

This assumption regarding prayer is reflected in the generic definitions commonly found in English-language dictionaries. *Webster's Third New International Dictionary of the English Language Unabridged,* to cite one example, defines prayer as "a solemn and humble approach to Divinity in word or thought." The indefiniteness of the term "Divinity" in this definition is apparently designed to suggest that prayer ought not to be limited to the act of any one religious group in addressing their particular god. Instead, the folks at Webster's are suggesting that all such acts, as well as similar utterances voiced by people addressing no god in particular, fall under the single rubric of prayer. Prayer, then, is supposedly not limited to any one religious tradition but is an experience that all people have in common. Understood in this manner,

---

1. Dietrich Bonhoeffer, *Letters and Papers from Prison,* ed. Eberhard Bethge, trans. Reginald H. Fuller (London: SCM, 1956), p. 67.

prayer is present among all societies and all peoples in the world. Perspectives such as these regarding the supposedly universal character of prayer have led some to conclude that prayer is natural, rooted in the instinctive recognition of one's dependence on a higher power.[2]

As significant as this insight into the basic human tendency to pray may be, the supposed universality of prayer does not provide the basis for the distinctively Christian understanding of this act. For this basis, we must direct our attention elsewhere — namely, to the development of prayer in the biblical communities of faith.

The Background to the Christian Concept of Prayer

Prayer may be in some sense an "instinctive" human experience. Yet, as Bonhoeffer's reluctance to offer Christian comfort to the man in the prison camp suggests, prayer often falls short of the specifically Christian understanding. In fact, biblical prayer differs in several respects from that found in many other ancient traditions. These differences may be illustrated by a comparison of the concept of the nature of prayer that arose among the Hebrews with that of ancient Greece.[3] Although Christian conceptions of prayer have from time to time been influenced by Greek ideas, the most significant background to the New Testament concept of prayer lies in the teaching of the Old Testament.

1. Prayer in the Greek Tradition

In Greece, prayer was regarded basically as the act of voicing one's requests to the various forces that can determine one's destiny. Because the power of the deities was seen as comprehensive, prayer was related to all aspects of human life. There was no activity or sphere of life that

2. See Albert Belden, *The Practice of Prayer* (New York: Harper & Brothers, n.d.), pp. 7-8; also, Harry Emerson Fosdick, *The Meaning of Prayer* (New York: Association Press, 1915), pp. 9-18.

3. See Heinrich Greeven, *"euchomai, euchē, proseuchomai, proseuchē,"* *Theological Dictionary of the New Testament*, ed. Gerhard Kittel, trans. Geoffrey Bromily, vol. 2 (Grand Rapids: Eerdmans, 1964), pp. 278-84.

should fail to be accompanied by sacrifices and prayers to the gods. Prayer, then, was motivated by a profound awareness of one's dependence on the gods.

Because the Greeks did not view the gods as being especially moral in character, they could not imagine that the deities could be swayed by moral considerations. For this reason, they approached the gods in a way that resembled the manner in which one would come into the presence of powerful princes. More specifically, they believed that prayer was to be accompanied by offerings and sacrifices, or by vows of the sacrifice the petitioner would offer should a favorable response be received. The Greeks petitioned the gods regarding concrete physical needs and for the purpose of soliciting their help in attaining specific goals. Petition was rarely connected to spiritual needs or needs pertaining to the inner person.

The Hellenistic period gave birth to two quite different ideas regarding prayer. The philosophical perspective, which typified the Stoics and the Cynics, was motivated by practical monotheism. These philosophers held no genuine belief in the many gods of the people. Instead, they acknowledged one god who they thought was basically impersonal. Consequently, they did not emphasize either petition as such or the idea that the petitioner should actually anticipate being heard. Seneca, for example, considered prayer for what a person could obtain for oneself to be foolish. Therefore, the philosophers rejected any idea that prayer is the cry of need to a god. Rather, they believed that it is designed to reflect the ideal toward which humans are to strive. This activity, they added, had value for the inner development of the person.

The second idea was popularized by the mystery religions. Lying behind this outlook was a quest for an experience of the presence of the deity, from whom the worshiper expected to receive salvation. Adherents of the mystery religions believed that prayer is a means to the vision of the divine. Because they deemed prayer to be significant insofar as it aided them in their quest for the experience of the gods, devotees of these religions considered the specific content of prayer unimportant. Moreover, they rarely offered petitions for the mundane things of life.

2. Prayer and the Old Testament

There are, of course, some similarities between the Old Testament concept of prayer and that of ancient Greece. Nevertheless, the two traditions differ greatly. Three features of the Old Testament understanding are especially noteworthy.[4]

First, in contrast to the practice of addressing prayers to many gods that permeated other ancient cultures, the Hebrews were taught to pray to the one God, Yahweh. Moreover, this God was known, for Yahweh had made himself the God of Israel and had constituted Israel as his people. For this reason the pray-er in Israel could approach God with the consciousness of being part of the community of God's people. Yahweh was known as well in that he had displayed his faithfulness toward his people. Thus the worshiper could approach Yahweh through a consciousness of his past actions. As John Wright has observed regarding the practice of prayer in the Old Testament, "Prayer, then, always carries this overtone of relationship to God initiated by his lovingkindness and sustained by his faithfulness."[5]

This aspect of ancient Hebrew prayer came to be developed further in the Christian community. Like Israel in the Old Testament, the church viewed prayer as a communal task that was based on a communal consciousness. When they prayed, the early Christians were conscious that they were part of the fellowship of people who belong to God through Jesus Christ. Likewise, the Old Testament idea of the faithfulness of God in the past continued to be a significant motivation for prayer for the early Christians. Yet, whereas the Old Testament community looked pre-eminently to the Exodus as the sign of God's faithfulness, the church underscored God's redemptive action in sending Christ. Then, as the centuries passed, signs of God's ongoing faithfulness became a continuing motivation for Christian prayer. The faithfulness of God in the past served as such an important impetus for prayer because it provided a signpost, pointing to and confirming God's promise of faithfulness in the present.

---

4. For summaries of the concept of prayer in the Old Testament, see John H. Wright, *A Theology of Christian Prayer* (New York: Pueblo, 1979), pp. 11-13; and Johannes Herrmann, *"euchomai* et al.," *Theological Dictionary of the New Testament,* vol. 2, pp. 785-800.

5. Wright, *A Theology of Christian Prayer,* p. 12.

In the Old Testament, prayer was addressed to the one God, Yahweh, who always remained *person*. The ancient Hebrews believed that Yahweh was the living sovereign who confronted his people in a personal way in both love and wrath.

This understanding gave rise to the question of God's willingness to hear prayer. The Hebrew pray-er earnestly sought to be heard. The crucial question became "How can I know that this active, loving, holy, living sovereign God gives ear to my petitions?" The ancient Hebrew petitioner knew that if Yahweh heard the prayer of his faithful servant, then the answer would surely come. For this reason as well, Old Testament prayers commonly appealed to Yahweh on the basis of his past actions and his promises of future assistance.

The final biblical answer to the question "Can I know that God hears my prayer?" came in John's first epistle: "This is the assurance we have in approaching God: that if we ask anything according to his will, he hears us. And if we know that he hears us — whatever we ask — we know that we have what we asked of him" (1 John 5:14-15). The bold assurance that John announces, however, raises a further question: What kind of prayer is in accordance with God's will? This important query forms the central topic of the subsequent chapters of this book.

Second, the Hebrew community believed that prayer encompassed all areas of life. In the Old Testament, requests were made to Yahweh regarding every aspect of existence, including the necessities of earthly life.[6] This emphasis arose in part out of the Hebrew perspective on the nature of the human person. Rather than assuming that the human person consists of a soul and a body that can be divided from each other, the ancient people of faith viewed the person as a substantial unity. The close connection between the physical and the spiritual indicative of this Hebrew way of thinking was evidenced even in prayer. The Hebrews did not consider petitioning God for physical needs unspiritual, because they knew that God is concerned for the whole person. This Old Testament viewpoint is evident, in turn, in the fourth petition of the Lord's Prayer: "Give us this day our daily bread." To ask for something as mundane as daily

---

6. Gauthier Adalbert Hamman, *Prayer: The New Testament* (Chicago: Franciscan Herald Press, 1971), p. 54.

bread is in keeping with God's concern for the whole person (see also Matt. 6:25-34).

One specific area of life loomed as especially crucial in Israel: the presence of the enemy. Because the Hebrews knew full well that they were surrounded by adversaries, prayer for deliverance from the enemy became prominent in the Old Testament. But the Hebrews added an interesting twist to this. Insofar as they were God's people, at stake in the struggle against the hostile nations was the cause of God itself,[7] for the enemies of Israel were in some sense the enemies of God.[8]

The theme of petition in the face of enemies is also reflected in Jesus' prayer: "Lead us not into temptation, but deliver us from the evil one." Just as the people of God in the Old Testament were surrounded by enemies and therefore prayed to God for deliverance, so also the disciples of the Lord are surrounded by the ultimate Enemy, the supremely Evil One. For this reason, prayer for deliverance continues to be vital and necessary throughout the church age (see also 1 Cor. 10:13).

The third feature of the Old Testament concept of prayer linked this activity to the worshiping life of the community.[9] Among the Hebrews, prayer was a communal act that was to be practiced within the context of worship. Moreover, this act was related to the sanctuaries of worship, especially the Jerusalem temple, which as the focal point of community religious life became central to prayer as well.

The story of Daniel's prayer as an exile in Babylon demonstrates this. Praying was not in and of itself problematic. On the contrary, everyone in Babylon was commanded to pray. What got Daniel thrown into the lions' den was his insistence on praying in one particular manner — namely, with his face directed toward Jerusalem. He prayed in this specific way because Jerusalem — or, more specially, the temple in Jerusalem — was the focal point for Hebrew prayer. His way of praying symbolized that he was directing his prayers toward Yahweh and Yahweh alone, not toward the king of the land to which he had been exiled.

7. Hamman, *Prayer: The New Testament*, p. 55.

8. Wayne R. Spear, *The Theology of Prayer* (Grand Rapids: Baker, 1979), p. 14. This position was not without its critics, however. During the exile, for example, the prophets spoke of Israel's enemies as agents of God's judgment on the covenant people.

9. Hamman, *Prayer: The New Testament*, pp. 55-56.

The central role of the temple for the Hebrew community finds its way into the New Testament as well, albeit with a crucial shift. At Pentecost a fundamental change was made in the economy of God: the church, the body of Christ, became the temple, which is now spiritual rather than physical or material. As a result, prayer can now be directed to God throughout the entire world. True prayer can be offered to God wherever the people of God find themselves, for they now are the new temple of the Holy Spirit, the symbol of God's earthly presence.

Because it was related to the worshiping life of the community, prayer in the Old Testament was related to the practice of offering sacrifices to God. In fact, the sacrifices of the people were to be accompanied by prayer.

Eventually, prayer overshadowed sacrifice as the central act of piety. This development began with the prophets, who placed great emphasis on an inner piety that was more pleasing to God than mere outward, ritual sacrifice. The trend toward elevating prayer to the center of Hebrew piety came to a climax after Israel was sent into exile.[10] This change was due in part to the physical separation from the temple that occurred when the Hebrews were deported from Palestine. When the people no longer lived in proximity to the temple, and eventually when the temple was destroyed, the prayer of the pious Jew took on increasing importance.

After the exile, the Jewish religious leaders developed specific forms of prayer and practiced regular times of prayer, although they continued to give place as well to extemporaneous prayer. This development formed a background to Jesus' interaction with the Pharisees on the topic of prayer. It is not the forms of prayer themselves that are important, Jesus declared, but the spirit or piety lying behind prayer.

Prayer and the Life of Jesus

The Old Testament concept of prayer forms an important background for the understanding of prayer in the New Testament faith community. Yet what provided the immediate context for the practice of prayer in the church was Jesus' teaching regarding prayer as well as his own

---

10. Hamman, *Prayer: The New Testament*, p. 54.

prayer life. Indeed, the disciples who became the pillars of the early church learned to pray at the feet of their Master.

1. Jesus: The Man of Prayer

Prayer was a central dimension of Jesus' life. All four Gospels, but especially Luke,[11] portray our Lord as a person of prayer. The centrality of prayer for Jesus is evident in the amount of time that he spent alone in prayer. Repeatedly, the Evangelists picture him withdrawing from the crowds in order to be alone with his Father. In fact, Jesus' ministry oscillated between engagement and disengagement. He was alternately with the people, teaching and healing, and alone with his heavenly Father for times of prayer. Occasionally, Jesus spent extended periods of time in prayer — "forty days" or "all night." Or he would rise before daybreak to pray. As David Stanley concludes regarding Luke's portrait of the Master, "A habit of prayer is made an important and constant feature of Jesus' ministry."[12]

The Gospels indicate that the signs and wonders Jesus performed were often preceded by prayer.[13] For example, before he called forth Lazarus from the grave, Jesus prayed to the Father. Similarly, before feeding the five thousand, Jesus blessed the loaves and fish.

The Gospels underscore the importance of prayer at crucial stages in Jesus' life. One such occasion was his baptism. David Stanley outlines the significance of this event for Luke's portrayal of Jesus' life:

> Thus it is of set purpose that Luke presents Jesus, at his first appearance in the narrative of his public life immediately after his baptism by John, as engaged in prayer. . . . The reader is alerted concerning the significant role prayer is to play in Jesus' mission as Messiah at the very moment when he is anointed with the Spirit and acknowledged as Son by the Father. Luke appears to imply moreover that this theophany happens precisely in answer to that prayer.[14]

11. See David M. Stanley, *Jesus in Gethsemane* (New York: Paulist, 1980), pp. 188-93.
12. Stanley, *Jesus in Gethsemane*, p. 190.
13. Stanley, *Jesus in Gethsemane*, p. 191.
14. Stanley, *Jesus in Gethsemane*, p. 189.

A similar event occurred prior to the selection of the twelve apostles. Luke highlights the crucial role played by prayer in this momentous decision.[15] Jesus made his choices during an all-night vigil in which he seemed actually to weigh the matter carefully in prayer before his heavenly Father.

Prayer was important at Jesus' transfiguration as well. Indeed, Jesus' purpose in ascending the mountain was to pray (Luke 9:28-29). The lengthy time of prayer that Jesus enjoyed while the disciples slept occasioned the extraordinary change in his appearance that they later witnessed.[16]

Times of intensive prayer also preceded Jesus' battles with Satan. Matthew and Luke speak of a forty-day period of fasting and prayer in the wilderness prior to the coming of the tempter. The night before Jesus' crucifixion was also an important occasion for prayer. Jesus not only interceded for his disciples, who would become the targets of the devil's challenge (e.g., John 17); he also struggled in prayer in Gethsemane as he faced impending betrayal and death.

Finally, prayer was significant even on the cross. Jesus' prayer of dereliction, "My God, my God, why have you forsaken me?" (Matt. 27:46), changed to the prayers of victory: "It is finished!" (John 19:30) and "Father, into your hands I commit my spirit" (Luke 23:46).

Jesus clearly was a person of prayer.

2. Jesus' Attitude in Prayer

Jesus was not only a man of prayer; he also displayed an exemplary attitude toward prayer. In his prayer life, Jesus indicated a unique relationship with his Father. This awareness is reflected in his preferred means of addressing his Father: *Abba.* The Gospel writers often prefer to leave the term untranslated, in the original Aramaic, which was the common language of Palestine in Jesus' day. The word itself is a term of endearment that expresses close familial ties. Preachers are fond of asserting that *Abba* is equivalent to the English designation "Daddy." In fact, however, *Abba* does not carry the overtones of a small child addressing a parent that are evoked by the English "Daddy." As the New Testament

15. Stanley, *Jesus in Gethsemane*, p. 190.
16. Stanley, *Jesus in Gethsemane*, p. 191.

scholar James Barr points out, rather than carrying the idea of "Daddy," the word "was more a solemn, responsible, adult address to a Father."[17] Hence, *Abba* is likely closer to our idea of "Dad."

In any case, the bond, the unparalleled closeness that Jesus sensed with his heavenly *Abba,* produced in him a certainty of being heard in prayer. In this way, Jesus' relationship with his Father provided the fulfillment of the quest for certainty that was so significant among the ancient Hebrews. Jesus' certainty of being heard is evident in the prayer that he voiced prior to raising Lazarus: "Father, I thank you that you have heard me. I knew that you always hear me, but I said this for the benefit of the people standing here, that they may believe that you sent me" (John 11:41b-42).

Jesus' sense that he enjoyed a unique relationship with his heavenly *Abba* included a strong belief that the Father acknowledged him and his mission. Jesus claimed that he had been sent by God. This deep sense of divine vocation led to, and was reflected in, his boldness in prayer. Gauthier Adalbert Hamman has encapsulated well this aspect of Jesus' attitude:

> Every situation, every petition always brought Jesus back to the object of his mission, the divine will, the work his Father had entrusted to him. Jesus desired nothing else. Prayer enabled him to discern and bless the plan of his Father whom he had come to serve. His petitions had no objects other than the good will of the Father and the will to act in his service.
>
> Therefore he could give thanks before a miracle; since his Father always granted what he asked, his will being entirely in accord with that of God. This submission motivated his filial and absolute trust.[18]

In his prayer life, Jesus also evidenced a profound sense of the importance of intercession. Our Lord regularly interceded for his disciples — his friends (e.g., John 17). But he also beseeched his heavenly Father on behalf of his enemies, his persecutors, and even those who put him to death. As he was being nailed to the cross, Jesus cried out, "Father,

---

17. Barr, "'Abba' Isn't 'Daddy,'" *Journal of Theological Studies* 39, no. 1 (April 1988): 46.
18. Hamman, *Prayer: The New Testament,* p. 182.

forgive them, for they do not know what they are doing" (Luke 23:34). According to Jesus, then, intercession is not to be exclusivistic; it is not to be offered only for those to whom we sense a close bond. Rather, he indicated that prayer is to bubble over to the world and even to those who oppose us. By praying in this manner, he stands as a living example of his well-known teaching, "Love your enemies and pray for those who persecute you" (Matt. 5:44).

Jesus' prayer life indicates as well that he viewed prayer as an eschatological activity — that is, he saw prayer as being connected to the final completion of God's work in the world. This is not surprising. Jesus understood his entire mission in the same light. He knew full well that he had come to announce and inaugurate God's rulership over all creation, including humankind. For him, prayer was one of the means by which this mission was to be accomplished.

We find in Jesus' life two ways in which he directed his praying toward the completion of God's work. First, Jesus viewed prayer as a focal point in his battle against Satan. Prayer was a means by which he came to be equipped to gain the victory over God's cosmic foe. This is evident already at the beginning of his ministry. The extended period of fasting and prayer that followed Jesus' baptism prepared the Master to withstand the Satanic onslaught during the temptation in the wilderness (Matt. 4:1-11; Luke 4:1-13). The close of his ministry witnessed a similar battle. Alone in Gethsemane, Jesus defeated his enemy, who tempted him to avoid the cross. This great cosmic victory came by means of fervent prayer (Mark 14:32-42 and parallel texts).

Prayer was not merely the means for preparation for battle. Jesus found prayer helpful in a second manner as well. He repeatedly directed prayer toward the One who one future day would bring the kingdom in its fullness, the One whose rule would come at the end of the age as the divine gift of grace. We dare not overlook the significance of this: In the midst of an evil generation and while facing the evils of life in this age, the Son of God prays — beseeches the Father — that the kingdom come. We might suggest that in this sense prayer was Jesus' own cry for the kingdom. As such it was for him an eschatological activity, a petitioning of the Sovereign God of history to bring the divine program for history to its glorious goal — namely, the kingdom of God.

Seeing Jesus' prayer as an eschatological activity, as a cry for the kingdom, provides the context for understanding the petitions of the

Lord's Prayer. The initial requests — "hallowed be your name, your kingdom come, your will be done on earth as it is in heaven" — form one overarching petition that is then elaborated in the subsequent supplications. The requests for sustenance, forgiveness, and deliverance are the marks of the presence of the kingdom among us. In this manner, the entire prayer becomes a single petition for the in-breaking of the kingdom into the present.

The cry for God's gracious provision reaches a climax in the request for God's Spirit. As the herald of the kingdom, Jesus was endowed with the Spirit's fullness. Consequently, he never petitioned the Father to send the Spirit of power on himself. But because the disciples were to share in this endowment, he declared that the Father would respond to their request for this eschatological gift: "How much more will your Father in heaven give the Holy Spirit to those who ask him!" (Luke 11:11-13). David Willis correctly points out the significance of this petition: "The Holy Spirit is the best of all that God the heavenly Father wills for his children. The Spirit is that special gift which enables them to try to live appropriately in the kingdom's presence."[19]

3. Jesus' Prayer and the Church

Although he was a man of intense prayer, Jesus did not limit his prayer life to himself. Even though he repeatedly petitioned God on his own behalf, his praying — like every aspect of his life and ministry — was ultimately for the sake of others. His followers readily realized that he intended to share his prayer life with them and, by extension, with the church as a whole. Moreover, this prayer connection linking Jesus with his body, the church, was not limited to his earthly sojourn. Rather, it continues throughout the church age until his return in glory. Jesus' ministry of prayer encompasses the church in several ways.

First, Jesus' prayer enfolds the church insofar as he intercedes for his followers. This was the case when Jesus walked the streets of Palestine. The most complete glimpse we have into this aspect of Jesus' earthly ministry occurs in what is often called Jesus' high-priestly prayer, which he voiced in the upper room on the night before his cru-

---

19. Willis, *Daring Prayer* (Atlanta: John Knox, 1977), p. 55.

cifixion. Although the primary focus of his intercession was the first disciples, Jesus extended the circle of the prayer to include the entire church: "My prayer is not for them alone [i.e., those present in the upper room]. I pray also for those who will believe in me through their message" (John 17:20).

Rather than coming to an end at his death, this ministry of intercession continues. The resurrected Lord has ascended to "the right hand of the Father," where, as the believers' advocate with the Father (1 John 2:1), he intercedes on behalf of his own (Rom. 8:34). Actually, intercession is the only aspect of the Lord's direct work on our behalf that the New Testament writers declare continues after the close of his earthly ministry (Heb. 7:25).

Jesus' prayer enfolds the church likewise through the presence of the Comforter among them and through their use of *Abba* in prayer. Jesus promised his disciples that after his departure he would send "another comforter," the Holy Spirit, to dwell within each believer and in the church (John 14:16-17). Paul perceived in this promise a far-reaching implication for prayer: By this Spirit, believers now cry *"Abba,* Father," after the pattern of Jesus' own prayers (Rom. 8:15; Gal. 4:6). The prerogative to address God in this manner indicates that the close relationship Jesus enjoyed with the Father has been given to his people, a relationship mediated by the presence of the Spirit. This closeness is revealed in the conversation that believers are invited to share with Jesus' heavenly Father.

Paul's insight into the believing community's familial relationship to God arises naturally from the address found in the Lord's Prayer. In giving this prayer to his disciples, Jesus authorized them to repeat the divine address, *Abba,* after him. And following his example, they are invited to speak in a familiar, trusting way, as a child does with his — and their — caring, heavenly Father.

Some people today recoil at the idea of calling God *"Abba,* Father." They point out that "father" is not a positive term for those whose earthly fathers were absent or abusive. And the exclusive use of this designation, they add, fails to give place to the symbolism of God as mother that is also found in Scripture. We dare not dismiss objections such as these in a cavalier manner. Those who voice them are attempting to provide an important corrective to the widely held but erroneous assumption that God is male.

At the same time, the hesitancy to address God as *"Abba,* Father" all too often overlooks the profundity of the privilege that this prerogative entails. Prayer is not offered to God as Father because God is male or because God is in every way like an earthly father. Rather, we come to God in this manner solely at the invitation of Jesus. As our elder brother, Jesus offers to us the privilege of addressing God by the designation "Father" as a sign of our participation through him in God's spiritual family. Through Jesus, we come into the presence of the One whom he called *"Abba,* Father." Hence, to address God by means of this designation is to revel in the relationship that Jesus enjoyed with God. It is to express the good news that through Jesus the pray-er has become a sister or a brother of Jesus and a co-heir with the Son.

One further consideration ought to be noted as well. The God revealed by Jesus is the loving, concerned, personal God who cares for all creation and for everyone. Rather than supporting a paternalistic, abusive understanding of human fatherhood, therefore, addressing God as Father actually does the opposite. It calls to judgment all ungodly human paternalisms. It demands that all human fathers measure themselves against the revealed nature of God. And it offers a relationship with one who is truly Father to those whose family experience has left them fatherless.

David Willis states the matter well when he declares, "It belongs to our growth to say 'abba' of God. For in doing so, we are saying that, despite evidence to the contrary, we trust that the world is ultimately a benevolent and purposeful realm."[20] Willis finds Jesus' description of God as "heavenly" to be of great consequence in this respect:

> "Heavenly" when used of God as father is a description of priorities, not primarily of location. "Heavenly" points not to where God is but to how much more God is than earthly fathers. "Heavenly" refers to the extra of God as father which goes *beyond* our experiences of earthly fatherhood.[21]

This suggests a third manner in which Jesus' life of prayer enfolds the community of his followers. He invites us to use his name in

---

20. Willis, *Daring Prayer,* p. 51.
21. Willis, *Daring Prayer,* pp. 54-55.

prayer (John 14:13; 16:24; cf. James 5:14). To pray in Jesus' name is a multifaceted privilege. It indicates that in prayer we are privy to the power of Jesus himself. Although this concept is foreign to our understanding, in ancient culture knowing the name of a person carried great meaning. It entailed the ability to tap into that person's power. In the biblical imagery, then, using the name of Jesus in prayer means that we are privileged to draw from his power in the presence of God.

To pray in the name of Jesus also involves praying in the place of Jesus. By using Jesus' name we are declaring that the prayer we are voicing is what Jesus would pray if he himself were speaking.

In addition, praying in Jesus' name entails sensing a oneness with the Lord as his sister or brother. Such prayer comprises an implicit acknowledgment that we have access to the Father only through Jesus the Son. And it allows us to share in Jesus' certainty of being heard. We know that the Father hears us because we are approaching the throne of grace solely through the Son, Jesus.

Moreover, by praying in the name of Jesus, we are joining our prayer to the prayer of Jesus. Because our prayer is joined to Jesus' prayer through the use of his name, our praying, like his, becomes an eschatological activity. As Theodore Jennings rightly declared, joining in prayer with Jesus means

> to join in the plea for God, in the call for God which "takes the kingdom by violence." It is protesting every barrier between ourselves and God, protesting our godlessness and godforsakenness and asking God that his name be hallowed, his kingdom come, his goal accomplished, "on earth as it is in heaven."[22]

Finally, Jesus' prayer life comes to encompass the church as we follow his example. As I noted previously, Jesus' example includes praying for one's enemies. Therefore, to petition the Father on behalf of those who oppose the gospel and who persecute the church is to imitate Jesus himself.

Above all, we follow Jesus' example as we pattern our prayer after

---

22. Jennings, *Life as Worship: Prayer and Praise in Jesus' Name* (Grand Rapids: Eerdmans, 1982), p. 27.

the model that he gave to his disciples — the Lord's Prayer. This prayer opens a window into the very mind and heart of Jesus himself.

In some Christian traditions, the reciting of this prayer has become a central aspect of both individual and communal supplication. Other Christians prefer not to use the prayer itself as a regular part of their public or private spiritual life. More important than whether or not we actually repeat the words of the Lord's Prayer is the quest to be faithful to the teaching regarding the spirit and content of prayer found therein. By this model prayer, Jesus emphasizes the importance of having a proper attitude, motivation, and intent when coming to the Father. As his disciples are conscious of the communal nature of all petitioning, seek above all the hallowing of the Father's name, and cry for the in-breaking of the kingdom into the brokenness of the present, the prayer of Jesus truly becomes their own.

The Lord's Prayer, therefore, stands as the capstone of Jesus' prayer life shared with us. For this reason, when we pattern our prayer after his, our prayer becomes an eschatological activity. Just as the petition "Your kingdom come, your will be done on earth as it is in heaven" formed the heart of Jesus' praying, so also in every situation the petitions of Jesus' friends ought to be a cry for the in-breaking of God's rulership, God's will, into our world. Gabriel Daly's remark is surely correct: "Every truly Christian prayer of petition is, implicitly at least, a request that the Kingdom may come."[23] In short, like Jesus' own prayer, Christian prayer is ultimately a cry for the kingdom.

Prayer in the New Testament Church

Conscious that he had shared his prayer life with them, Jesus' followers applied the Master's teaching regarding prayer to the various situations they faced. The perspective on prayer that developed in the early church, in turn, came to be inscripturated in the epistles of the New Testament.

The English language offers merely one central term to designate prayer. But the New Testament writers found a variety of Greek words to highlight the various aspects of this activity. Some of these terms re-

---

23. Daly, *Asking the Father* (Wilmington, Del.: Michael Glazier, 1982), p. 80.

fer to prayer in general.[24] Others are more specifically related to the aspect of prayer that we call petition in general,[25] or intercession in particular.[26]

A quick overview of the variety of words that the New Testament authors drew upon to speak about prayer leads to two significant observations about the understanding of prayer in the early church. First, with few exceptions[27] the words that the biblical writers chose to refer to prayer were normal, "run-of-the-mill" words of the day. They were used by first-century Greek-speaking people to refer to communication on a human level. This suggests that in the minds of the New Testament authors, prayer to God was not something that differed radically from human communication. Rather, in their estimation, prayer to God is by its very nature analogous to the discourse that takes place in the day-in and day-out living of ordinary folks.

Second, the New Testament authors place a great emphasis on

24. Thus *euchē*, a noun, and its related verb, *euchomai*, although often used as merely secular terms meaning "wish" (Acts 27:29; 3 John 2; Rom. 9:3) or "vow" (Acts 18:18; 21:23), are occasionally used to refer to prayer (as a noun, James 5:15; as a verb, Acts 26:29; 2 Cor. 13:7, 9; James 5:16). A second pair of terms is related to the first: *proseuchē* (noun) and *proseuchomai* (verb). The New Testament writers prefer these terms over the root word because they are devoid of the basically secular meaning carried by *euchē*. These words denote prayer in a comprehensive fashion, although on occasion they are used in the stricter sense of "petition."

25. *Aitēma* and its related verb, *aiteō*, are the normal Greek words for "ask" or "request." These terms are used to refer to asking in prayer as well (Matt. 21:22; Phil. 4:6; 1 John 5:15). *Erōtaō* is most generally used in a secular sense, e.g., "to ask a question" (Matt. 16:13) or "to make a request" (Luke 7:3). John, however, utilizes this term to refer to prayer (1 John 5:16). *Deēsis* and its related verb, *deomai*, mean "supplication." The noun is always used in the religious sense in the New Testament. The verb form, however, can also carry a secular meaning.

26. *Enteuxis*, which is perhaps related to the verb *entynchanō*, means "intercession." The verb, which is used in both a secular and a religious sense, originally meant, according to Trench, "to fall in with a person, to draw close to him so as to enter into familiar speech and communion with him." See Richard Chenevix Trench, *Synonyms of the New Testament* (Grand Rapids: Eerdmans, 1953), p. 190. The noun refers to "free familiar prayer" — that is, that kind of intercession which results from communion with someone well known. Several other terms round out the list: *Parakaleō* and the related verb *epikaleomai* are on occasion used in the sense of "call." The term *eulogeō* refers to grace at mealtime. "Give thanks" is the meaning of *eucharisteō*. Finally, *krazō* carries the meaning of "cry" — that is, "cry out to God."

27. The most significant is *proseuchomai*.

petitionary prayer. Petitioning God is not the only element present in New Testament prayer, but it is a vital element.

This may seem surprising to us today. Indeed, it forms a stark contrast to a tendency prevalent in the last two hundred years to view petition as a lowlier type of prayer. Many Christian teachers suggest that as believers mature, their prayers move away from the "beggarly" activity of asking God to intervene in human situations and to provide for human needs. These teachers imply that Christians who are truly mature replace petitionary prayer with the desire simply to "be with" or "commune with" God. The widely enjoined emphasis on communion with God elevates adoration and thanksgiving above petition.

Adoration and thanksgiving — indeed, the desire simply to commune with God — are, of course, vital in prayer. Yet the New Testament writers seem to move in another direction. The Scriptures indicate that the Christian ought never to "mature" beyond petitionary prayer. The mature spiritual person never outgrows the need to bring requests to God. The position of the entire New Testament may be summarized by Paul's word to the Philippians: "Rejoice in the Lord always. . . . Do not be anxious about anything, but in everything, by prayer and petition, with thanksgiving, present your requests to God" (Phil. 4:4-6). David M. Stanley encapsulates the Pauline view in this way: "Prayer, as man's response to the divine graciousness, must retain its essentially petitionary character with recurring sentiments of joy and thanksgiving."[28]

This emphasis on petition indicates that the New Testament writers continued the eschatological orientation of prayer that they saw in Jesus' own outlook. Like the Master, they present prayer as an eschatological activity, the petitioning for the coming of the kingdom into the present. By beseeching God for divine provision in the midst of the brokenness and insufficiency of the present, the Christian community seeks the power of the Spirit for its task of continuing the ministry of the risen Lord, until he returns in glory (see 2 Pet. 3:11-12). By petitioning God in the midst of the present experience of persecution and evil that the righteous Judge return in judgment and vindication, the church anticipates the final day of the Lord. In short, the New Testament writers describe the prayer of the community of faith as the cry for the kingdom.

---

28. Stanley, *Boasting in the Lord* (New York: Paulist, 1973), pp. 180-83.

According to the New Testament, petition can be voiced boldly because of the presence of the two great eschatological signposts: the resurrection of Jesus and the presence of the Holy Spirit. These events encourage the faithful community to petition God to bring about the completion of God's work in the world, in the church, and in the life of each believer. In the New Testament church, the hope of the consummation lay behind all petition, as the early Christians sought to know Christ "and the power of his resurrection" (Phil. 3:10). They realized that all of life is a call by God "heavenward in Christ Jesus" (Phil. 3:14). This awareness shaped and was shaped by the prayer life of the early community.

Christian Prayer and the Church of All Ages

Following in the footsteps of the New Testament writers, Christians in every age have reflected on and sought to understand the nature of prayer. In recent years, some scholars, especially those whose discipline is the philosophy of religion, have attempted to understand Christian prayer as a variety of a more general human phenomenon. Friedrich Heiler, to cite one example, concluded his classic study of the varied phenomena of prayer in the religious traditions of the world with a basic definition of the essence of prayer. He attempted to define prayer "in its primitive simplicity" — that is, as what "the simple, devout person, undisturbed by reflection" thinks during prayer. Heiler concluded, "Prayer is, therefore, a living communion of the religious man with God, conceived as personal and present in experience, a communion which reflects the forms of the social relations of humanity."[29] Speaking from a more self-consciously Christian perspective, Perry LeFevre calls prayer "the means by which God acts through human freedom in the present to transform personal and social existence toward the kingdom of God."[30]

The discussion that has led us to this point suggests a somewhat

29. Heiler, *Prayer* (New York: Oxford University Press, 1932), pp. 353-58.

30. LeFevre, *Radical Prayer: Contemporary Interpretations* (Chicago: Exploration Press, 1982), pp. 84-85. For a quite different understanding based on the teachings of the church fathers, see Robert L. Simpson, *The Interpretation of Prayer in the Early Church* (Philadelphia: Westminster, 1965), pp. 154-57.

more straightforward and simple description of the nature of prayer: Prayer is direct communication with God. Christian prayer, in turn, is the cry for the kingdom. What remains is to round out the chapter by setting forth a general understanding of Christian prayer as a practice present in the church in every era.

At its heart, prayer entails communion with God. It involves a sense of the presence of God. But prayer as communion with God goes beyond the mere enjoyment of God's presence. Rather, prayer is the activity of communicating with the God in whose presence we exist. This activity presupposes a standing-over-against Another, a relationship of the pray-er to the One addressed in prayer.[31]

Understood as communication with God, prayer moves in two directions. It includes both the human person speaking to God and God speaking to the human person. The New Testament suggests that prayer in the sense of humans speaking to God consists of four aspects, which together, therefore, constitute a well-rounded prayer life. These dimensions form an acrostic with the word ACTS: Adoration, Confession, Thanksgiving, and Supplication.

The first aspect, *adoration,* entails praising God for who God is. This is in keeping with the Lord's Prayer, which begins, "Our Father in heaven, hallowed be your name" (Matt. 6:9). Adoration is hallowing or making holy the name of God. This aspect of prayer centers on the nature of God. The pray-er praises God because of God's perfect character.

Some teachers have questioned the propriety of adoration in prayer. They wonder why the eternal God would be needful of or even desirous of the continual acclamation of sinful, finite creatures. The British theologian Norman Pittenger has offered an intriguing response to this question: "Doubtless God himself does not 'enjoy' continual praise, but he 'puts up with it' because he knows it is good for his human children." Further reflection then led Pittenger to voice an even deeper consideration: "If God really is a Lover, he must delight in having those whom he loves respond to him in love and want to be with

31. See A. Raymond George, *Communion with God in the New Testament* (London: Epworth Press, 1953). This is similar to George's second type of piety, which speaks of God in the second person and differs from mystical absorption into the divine (p. 12). George shows that the prayer practiced and taught by Jesus was of this prophetic type (pp. 114-15).

him and tell him their love."[32] In this way Pittenger offered two important understandings of the significance of adoration. Offering praise to God is beneficial to the pray-er, insofar as adoration is a safeguard against idolatry and false pride. At the same time, God delights in the praise of God's people, for such adoration symbolizes the human response of love to the gracious Creator and Redeemer.

The second aspect of prayer, *confession,* might be described as the acknowledgment of our own sinfulness and an expression of agreement with God regarding it. Both ingredients in confession are important. Not only is it important that we admit our sinfulness, but we must also agree with God that sin is abhorrent.

In the Lord's Prayer, Jesus encouraged confession. His model prayer includes the petition "Forgive us our sins" (Luke 11:4). Matthew follows the giving of this prayer with a comment from the Lord regarding the relationship between divine and human forgiveness: "For if you forgive [others] when they sin against you, your heavenly Father will also forgive you. But if you do not forgive [others] their sins, your Father will not forgive your sins" (Matt. 6:14-15). The Old Testament emphasizes the importance of confession as well. Confession is a prerequisite to the reception of God's provision (e.g., Jer. 5:25; Ps. 66:18) and God's word. God's messenger came to Daniel, for example, while Daniel was "speaking and praying, confessing my sin and the sin of my people Israel" (Dan. 9:20).

Adoration and confession form a natural progression. As we come to see God in God's glory, we are confronted with our own shortcomings and failures. Isaiah experienced this progression. As he saw the Lord "high and lifted up" and the angels singing "Holy, holy, holy is the LORD," he was brought to an awareness of his sin and the sin of his people (Isa. 6:1-6).

The third aspect of the human conversation with God is *thanks-*

---

32. Pittenger, *Praying Today* (Grand Rapids: Eerdmans, 1974), p. 56. Heiler's study of the nature of prayer resulted in different conclusions concerning the place of adoration in the life of prayer. He understood adoration in terms of reverent contemplation and so defined it as "the solemn contemplation of the 'Holy One' as the highest Good, unreserved surrender to Him, a mingling of one's being with His." Although this activity together with devotion "are absolutely necessary elements in religious experience," he concluded that these are "more general religious phenomena: which ought not be confused with the essence of prayer" (Heiler, *Prayer,* pp. 353-58).

giving, the act of expressing gratitude to God for what God has done and is doing (1 Thess. 5:18). Thanksgiving differs from adoration in that the former focuses on the nature and character of God, whereas the latter is a response to what God does on behalf of the church and the world. Thanksgiving arises from the reception of God's gifts; adoration focuses on the Giver.[33] Thanksgiving is a natural outgrowth of confession. As believers acknowledge their sinfulness and receive the forgiveness of God (1 John 1:9), the experience of being forgiven results in a thankful heart.

The final dimension of prayer is *supplication.* This includes petitioning God on behalf of the needs of others (1 Thess. 5:25) as well as one's own needs (Phil. 4:6). This aspect of prayer will emerge as the central topic of the subsequent chapters of this volume.

Prayer involves speaking to God. It also entails listening for God to speak. The Bible emphasizes by precept and example the importance of listening. Because each listened, Peter received a divine vision (Acts 10:9-10), the church in Antioch heard the voice of the Spirit (Acts 13:2), Paul was directed to Macedonia (Acts 16:9), and John the seer received a revelation of Jesus Christ (Rev. 1:9-10).

Listening for God is closely related to the Old Testament practice of waiting on the Lord. Isaiah declares, "But those who hope in the LORD will renew their strength" (Isa. 40:31). The verb translated "hope" in this text actually means "to bind together" and thus "to expect." It speaks of "looking patiently," "tarrying," "waiting for," and "waiting upon." In another context the prophet declares, "Blessed are all who wait for him" (Isa. 30:18). Waiting on the Lord includes silent anticipation of God speaking.

This aspect of prayer, listening to and receiving from God, is a reminder that ultimately prayer is initiated not by the pray-er but by God. William Meninger outlines the implications of this:

> Prayer begins with God, not with us. . . . The invitation has to come from God — what comes from us is the response.
>
> When we "begin to pray" or think we are beginning to pray, we should be explicitly aware that, whether we are emotionally aware of

---

33. For a similar distinction, see *The Great Christian Doctrines,* ed. James Hastings (Edinburgh: T&T Clark, 1915), p. 133. See also Wright, *A Theology of Christian Prayer,* pp. 58-61.

it or not, God has initiated this prayer. The invitation has already come from Him, the prayer has already begun, the grace is present and all we have to do is respond![34]

These sentiments have been echoed by Robert L. Simpson:

> God is the *transcendent* Referent of prayer in yet another sense. The effects of prayer, the movement of prayer, are not the result of human initiative; rather, prayer begins with God. As the fathers indicate, God provides the form, the content, and the power of prayer; hence its very possibility. Thus we assert that prayer itself is a gift of grace, that it wells up in the context of grace.[35]

An effective and well-rounded prayer life must include both directions of the communication that is prayer. The people of God are to seek to communicate with the Eternal One, speaking words of adoration, confession, thanksgiving, and supplication. Moreover, they are to "wait upon the Lord," seeking to receive divine consolation, strength, and instruction in return. As in other activities of the Christian life, through prayer, God's people sense God's presence among them. In this way they not only cry for the kingdom but also come to enjoy a foretaste of the eschatological kingdom in the midst of the brokenness of the present age.

34. Meninger, "Aspects of Prayer," in *Word and Spirit: A Monastic Review* (Still River, Mass.: St. Bede's Publications, 1982), pp. 147-49.

35. Simpson, *The Interpretation of Prayer in the Early Church*, pp. 165-66.

2. How Petitionary Prayer "Works"

The previous chapter concluded with an acrostic that described prayer as consisting of four aspects. Christians generally have little problem with the idea of prayer as long as only the first three of these — adoration, confession, and thanksgiving — are in view. Most believers readily acknowledge the propriety of these forms of prayer. In fact, they might even extol the benefits that come as people offer such prayers to God. Similarly, Christians generally grant that the reverse side of communicating with God — listening silently in God's presence — is also important, even if they do not give much attention to the practice of this discipline themselves.

Difficulties arise, however, when we move to the "s" in the acrostic of prayer: supplication. Some Christians go so far as to question the validity of this activity. Others willingly admit that the Bible emphasizes petitionary prayer, but find that they simply do not engage in this practice consistently. Many of these believers do not pray as they know they should because they are not convinced that prayer makes any difference. They doubt that petitioning God really "works." Such people are often not convinced *that* prayer works, in turn, simply because they do not understand *how* prayer works.

The goal of this chapter is to seek to rectify this difficulty by engaging with the "how" question: How does supplication work? I want to seek to discover what happens when we pray. Motivating these reflections is my conviction that as we come to understand what God intends to happen when we pray, we will engage in this crucial discipline of the Christian life more effectively. Or, to state the point in another manner, as we come to pray with greater understanding, prayer will take on greater meaning in our lives.

What Supplication "Effects"

Before we can think through the manner in which prayer works, however, we must gain a sense about what prayer is intended to do. The way to begin this voyage of discovery is by surveying the biblical writings. Our goal here is to determine what the authors of Scripture indicate are the intended effects of petition. Such a survey reveals that these effects run in four directions: petition can affect those who petition God for their own needs, those on behalf of whom prayer is offered, the host of spiritual forces in the cosmos, and even God. Let's look at each of these in turn.

First, the Scriptures indicate that prayer is intended to affect the one who prays, the "pray-er" who petitions God in the midst of his or her own sense of need. Indeed, praying for ourselves can occasion a variety of changes in our own lives.

One such change can be our own spiritual situation. Petition can effect personal salvation. Insofar as "everyone who calls upon the name of the Lord will be saved" (Rom. 10:12-13), God answers the prayer of the person who comes with the request for salvation. Petition can likewise occasion the fullness of the Spirit. Jesus promised that the Father would give the Holy Spirit to those who ask (Luke 11:13). Although this statement is perhaps best interpreted as referring to the reception of the Holy Spirit in salvation, other texts speak about the Spirit's filling of believers for service. For example, when the early church was commanded not to proclaim the message of Jesus Christ, its members petitioned God that they might be enabled to speak with boldness. Luke describes the Lord's response to this petition: "The place where they were meeting was shaken. And they were all filled with the Holy Spirit and spoke the word of God boldly" (Acts 4:31).

Petitioning God on our own behalf can bring about psychological change. Fear can be changed to boldness. The psalmist reported experiencing this kind of psychological or emotional transformation: "In my anguish I cried to the LORD, and he answered by setting me free" (Ps. 118:5). The psalmist then expressed the new boldness that came in response to prayer: "The LORD is with me; I will not be afraid. What can man do to me?" (v. 6; see also Ps. 138:3). Similarly, anxiety can give way to peace. Hence, Paul encourages the Philippian Christians to petition God so that this change can result: "Do not be anxious about anything, but in everything, by prayer and petition, with thanksgiving, present your requests to God. And the peace of God, which transcends all understanding, will guard your hearts and your minds in Christ Jesus" (Phil. 4:6-7).

The petitions of the pray-er can result in physical or material effects as well. The obscure Old Testament figure Jabez has in recent years become the most widely known example of such a prayer. Jabez cried out to God, "Oh, that you would bless me and enlarge my territory! Let your hand be with me, and keep me from harm so that I will be free from pain" (1 Chron. 4:10). What was the result? "And God granted his request."

I should note here that this Old Testament account reports what happened in one particular historical situation. This situation does not provide us with a universally applicable principle. Experiences from Paul's life indicate how different situations can yield very different results. On one occasion, Paul and Silas were miraculously freed from a Philippian prison in response to prayer (Acts 16:25-26). Yet Paul's repeated request that God remove what was likely a long-standing physical ailment (his "thorn in the flesh") was not granted (2 Cor. 12:7-9).

Second, we learn from Scripture that interceding on behalf of others can occasion effects in their lives. Such intercession can alter the spiritual situation of those for whom we pray. As the prayers found in Paul's epistles suggest, prayer can lead to the spiritual strengthening of and greater spiritual knowledge in others (e.g., Eph. 3:16-19; 2 Thess. 2:16-17; cf. Luke 22:32). This is evident, for example, in the manner in which the apostle intercedes for the Ephesian Christians:

> I pray that out of his glorious riches he may strengthen you with power through his Spirit in your inner being, so that Christ may dwell in your hearts through faith. And I pray that you, being rooted and established in love, may have power, together with all the saints, to grasp how wide and long and high and deep is the love of Christ, and to know this love that surpasses knowledge. (Eph. 3:16-19)

John adds that intercession can also result in forgiveness of sin and restoration of life: "If you see your brother or sister commit a sin that does not lead to death, you should pray and God will give them life" (1 John 5:16, NIV ILE).

Our intercession can also lead to an altered physical situation in the lives of those for whom we pray. According to James, this can include physical healing:

> Is any one of you sick? Call the elders of the church to pray over you and anoint you with oil in the name of the Lord. And the prayer offered in faith will make you well; the Lord will raise you up. If you have sinned, you will be forgiven. (James 5:14-15, NIV ILE)

James likewise cites the example of Elijah, whose prayers affected the weather in Israel (James 5:17-18). Similarly, Luke recounts how the intercession of the Jerusalem believers resulted in Peter's release from prison (Acts 12:5-7).

The Scriptures indicate that the effects of prayer can move in a third direction, namely, toward angels and demons. The book of Daniel recounts how angelic messengers were dispatched to God's servant in response to his prayers. Upon his arrival, the heavenly visitor declared to Daniel, "Since the first day that you set your mind to gain understanding and to humble yourself before your God, your words were heard, and I have come in response to them" (Dan. 10:12). The angel then suggested, however, that he had been involved in cosmic skirmish. Evil forces had hindered his journey to such an extent that he required the assistance of another heavenly being: "But the prince of the Persian kingdom resisted me twenty-one days. Then Michael, one of the chief princes, came to help me, because I was detained there with the king of Persia" (Dan. 10:13). The implication of the narrative is that Daniel's persistence in prayer was instrumental in the coming of Michael, leading to the release of the heavenly messenger.

Even more prominent in Scripture is the idea that demonic forces are affected by prayer. Jesus' own life demonstrates this, for prayer was repeatedly his resource in combating Satan. Matthew suggests that the forty days in the wilderness were a prayerful preparation for doing battle against the tempter (Matt. 4:1-11).

Other New Testament texts speak of the relationship between drawing near to God, which occurs in part by means of prayer, and overcoming Satan (e.g., James 4:7-8; 1 Pet. 5:8-9). Paul, for example, declares that the Christian's struggle is "not against flesh and blood, but against the rulers, against the authorities, against the powers of this dark world and against the spiritual forces of evil in the heavenly realm" (Eph. 6:12). Not only is wearing the proper armor crucial in this combat, but, Paul adds, prayer is indispensable. Consequently, he admonishes the Ephesians, "Pray in the Spirit on all occasions with all kinds of prayers and requests. With this in mind, be alert and always keep on praying for all the saints" (Eph. 6:18).

Jesus underscored the crucial role of prayer in dealing with demonic oppression in the incident following his transfiguration. Upon his return from the mountain with three of the disciples, he was confronted with the inability of the other nine to cast out a demon. After performing the exorcism, Jesus explained why they had been so spiritually impotent: "This kind can come out only by prayer" (Mark 9:29).

Despite the importance of these aspects of the intended effect of prayer, the central teaching of the Scriptures moves in a fourth direction: Petition can affect God.

The Old Testament narrates a variety of incidents in which prayer averted judgment from God. Jonah's proclamation to Nineveh is an example. The prophet did not want to preach to this enemy city because he knew that the repentance of its people would change God's intention and would avert destruction (Jon. 3:6-10). The principle that Jonah seemed to know well was articulated by Jeremiah: "If at any time I announce that a nation or kingdom is to be uprooted, torn down and destroyed, and if that nation I warned repents of its evil, then I will relent and not inflict on it the disaster I had planned" (Jer. 18:7-8).

Even more significant than the idea that prayer can avert divine judgment is the biblical depiction of petition as the means whereby God's power and willingness to act in a positive manner are released (e.g., Luke 11:11-13; John 16:24; Jer. 33:2-3; Ps. 86:7; 145:18; 2 Chron. 7:14). Jesus stated this principle by means of an analogy to human parents:

> Which of you fathers, if your son asks for a fish, will give him a snake instead? Or if he asks for an egg, will give him a scorpion? If you then, though you are evil, know how to give good gifts to your children, how much more will your Father in heaven give the Holy Spirit to those who ask him! (Luke 11:11-13)

In this analogy, our Lord drew from a basic characteristic of the parental heart. Children's requests release their parents' willingness and ability to shower them with good things. If the willingness of sinful parents to provide for their children is released by asking, Jesus declared, how much more does the petitioning by God's children release the power and willingness of their heavenly Father to provide for their good.

Prayer and Modern Psychology

The examples that I cited in the previous paragraphs indicate how prevalent in Scripture is the idea that petition brings results. Prayer can lead to change in the lives of those who pray for their own needs and in the lives of those for whom others intercede. Prayer can influence cosmic forces and spiritual beings. But above all, prayer can release divine action.

These observations raise the obvious question: How? How does petition effect such changes? How does prayer "work"? The attempt to understand the workings of prayer has not only challenged theologians; it has also become a crucial topic of psychology.

1. Prayer as Molding Our Will to the Will of God

From its beginnings in the nineteenth century, modern psychology — especially the subfield of religious psychology — has drawn the study of prayer into its domain. Perhaps no one has had a more powerful impact on the psychological perspective on prayer than William James. In his widely read book *Varieties of Religious Experience,* James emphasizes the centrality of prayer to religion. Prayer, he says, "is the very soul and essence of religion."[1] James found prayer crucial to his study, insofar as this practice raises the question of the subjectivity of religious experience: Is prayer, and therefore all religious experience, only inner and personal, or does a genuine transaction occur between the one who prays and a transcendent God?

It is not surprising that the focal point of the attempt to answer

1. James, *The Varieties of Religious Experience* (New York: New American Library, 1958), p. 352.

this question has been petitionary prayer. Indeed, petition is a special stumbling block for modern, scientific accounts of how the universe functions.

For this reason, some psychologists have dismissed petition as "primitive." James himself offers this opinion of the prayer life of the famous nineteenth-century English evangelical George Mueller:

> George Mueller's is a case extreme in every respect, and in no respect more so than in the extraordinary narrowness of the man's intellectual horizon. His God was, as he often said, his business partner. He seems to have been for Mueller little more than a sort of supernatural clergyman interested in the congregation of tradesmen and others in Bristol who were his saints and in the orphanages and other enterprises, but unpossessed of any of those vaster and wilder and more ideal attributes with which the human imagination elsewhere has invested him. Mueller, in short, was absolutely unphilosophical. His intensely private and practical conception of his relations with the Deity continued the traditions of the most primitive human thought.[2]

Others have sought to overcome the difficulty bound up with petition by "spiritualizing" it or linking it with the development of inner piety. To this end, they narrow petitionary prayer to the search for purity of heart or patience in life's trials. Somewhat similar to the ancient Stoic philosophers, these scholars conclude that only requests directed to these ends ought to be voiced.

Yet no critique of petitionary prayer has been more consistently articulated than the idea that it suffers from a glaring and insurmountable difficulty. Petition, critics claim, sets up an irresolvable conflict between the divine will and the human will, between the goals of God and the desires of the petitioner. In this situation of the conflict of wills, they add, petitionary prayer is an attempt to bend the divine will in the direction of the human will. In short, when people pray, they are seeking to assert the will of the creature over the will of the Creator.[3]

---

2. James, *The Varieties of Religious Experience,* pp. 356-57.

3. Harry Emerson Fosdick attempts to counteract this position in *The Meaning of Prayer* (New York: Association Press, 1915). He writes, "Of all misconceptions of prayer, none is more common than the idea that it is a way of getting God to do our will" (p. 55).

In actual practice, many Christians embrace this understanding of prayer even though they might question it in theory. Some even go so far as to describe petition as a technique for bending the divine will to conform to the will of the petitioner.[4]

Most Christian psychologists and theologians, however, reject this kind of quasi-magical approach to prayer. In its place, some have suggested an understanding that moves in the opposite direction. Prayer, they postulate, is the attempt to submit one's will to the will of God. The famous nineteenth-century German theologian Friedrich Schleiermacher, for example, declared that prayer does not alter the course of events as ordained by God, but is a means of allaying our disquietude. In a similar manner, his philosophical counterpart, Immanuel Kant, asserted that prayer serves to establish in the petitioner the disposition to obey God.

The proposals of Schleiermacher and Kant have found echo in many conservative Christians. Many believers are convinced that the task of petitionary prayer is to mold the will of the individual to the will of God. Robert L. Simpson, for example, writes,

> The true significance of prayer within the framework of creative activity is this reshaping of the will by which the higher level of integrative interaction may proceed.
>
> Such an understanding of prayer reflects a transformation of the prayer of natural man, for Christian prayer aims not at the conformity of certain powers to human purposes but at the conformity of man to the demands or conditions by which higher degrees of related being may be achieved, by which "the purposes of God" may be realized.[5]

This outlook is correct as far as it goes. There is place for the prayer of surrender to the divine will, as is evidenced in Jesus' prayer in Gethsemane. Yet when this understanding is overemphasized, it readily dis-

---

4. This is noted by Donald G. Bloesch in *The Struggle of Prayer* (San Francisco: Harper & Row, 1980), p. 14.

5. Simpson, *The Interpretation of Prayer in the Early Church* (Philadelphia: Westminster, 1965), pp. 167, 172. See also Helen Jean Parks, *Holding the Ropes* (Nashville: Broadman Press, 1983), p. 23: "Prayer is not our asking God for things. It is God moving in us to pray for things he wants to do."

places another perspective on prayer that is more prevalent in the Bible. As the preceding survey reveals, the Scriptures repeatedly present prayer as bringing a response from God. Indeed, the central "prayer promise" of the New Testament seems to be "Whatever you ask in faith, you will receive." Consequently, we simply cannot reduce Christian prayer to the attempt to mold our will to the divine will, as important as this aspect of prayer is.

2. Prayer as Autosuggestion

Prayer is more than the molding of the will of the petitioner to the divine will. But if prayer does indeed bring about change, how can this be understood? Perhaps the most widely held psychological answer to this question could be encapsulated in the single word "autosuggestion." This theory claims that ultimately the actual object of petitionary prayer is not some higher being, but the pray-er.

For the philosophical basis of this proposal, we need to invoke again the name of Immanuel Kant. Kant inherited from his predecessors a profound sense of the limitations of human knowing. In fact, he drew this skeptical conclusion into the heart of his philosophical proposal. Kant declared that human scientific reason, which seeks to discover truth through the use of the senses, can yield no knowledge of any reality that transcends the realm of sense experience. One implication of this cautious attitude was the claim that prayer, which is supposedly addressed to God, is in fact a monologue. Kant readily admitted that the practice of prayer could bring certain results. What he denied was that these included actual intervention from a God who breaks into the chain of cause and effect within the orderly universe.[6] Viewed within Kant's framework, prayer can affect only the one who prays. Petition becomes autosuggestion.

The idea that prayer is autosuggestion provides what might at first glance appear to be a plausible explanation of the way in which peti-

---

6. There are several current variations on this basic view. John E. Biersdorf, for example, understands prayer as "reframing." He says it is a "dialogue between conscious mind and unconscious depths." See his *Healing of Purpose* (Nashville: Abingdon, 1985), pp. 126-28.

tion "works." Through prayer we are liberated to see ourselves. As we voice in prayer what we perceive our situation to be, we are enabled to see our various problems and difficulties more clearly. This clarity, in turn, helps us in the task of determining a proper course of action to deal with these problems. Furthermore, when we "bare our souls" before "God" in prayer, our true feelings come to the surface. We are enabled to admit the presence in us of feelings of guilt, inadequacy, and helplessness. Once pinpointed and acknowledged, these psychological hindrances can be overcome. Likewise, prayer frees us to put our finger on our real fears and anxieties, which in turn helps us in coping with them. The positive results of prayer then follow. Confusion is replaced by clear-sighted vision; fear is changed to boldness; anxiety gives way to peace; and feelings of inadequacy are replaced by self-confidence. This altered psychological situation leads to an altered physical situation, as the experience of release allows healing to occur. This, in turn, gives rise to well-being and personal success.

Viewing prayer as autosuggestion also provides a basis for understanding the impact that intercession can have on those for whom we pray. They are affected indirectly. Changes are brought about in their lives as an extension of the difference that prayer makes in ours. Praying for others challenges us to understand their problems, needs, and extenuating circumstances. So doing nurtures in us not only a sympathetic attitude toward them, but also the willingness to meet the very needs that we have voiced to "God" in our prayers. As those for whom we pray sense our sympathetic and understanding attitude, psychological renewal begins to occur in them. This clears the way for constructive engagement with their own situation. And motivated by our intercession, we assist in this process as we offer our direct aid to them in the task of meeting the problems that they are experiencing.

This understanding of the psychology of prayer lies at the heart of several contemporary attempts to describe the working of petition. For example, David Willis declares,

> Prayer does not change things. Prayer changes people who change things. . . . We move from an inward realization of acceptance to an outward behavioral validation of it. This is the opposite of struggling to prove ourselves in order to earn acceptance.
>
> . . . Taking to heart this acceptance by the Servant Lord sets us on

a road of service to others because it means that personal liberation is inseparable from becoming turned outward to the liberation of others.[7]

To his credit, Willis denies that his interpretation limits prayer to autosuggestion. He acknowledges that a higher being is indeed at work in this process:

> It is, of course, possible to say that psychological change through prayer occurs because of autosuggestion or because of the fundamental drawing power of an illusion. From a Christian perspective, however, this psychological change is not based on man's power of self-deception, ever-present as this element, of course, is in our imperfect faith. Our changed self-image is founded in the conviction that God's correction and acceptance of us preceded and overruled any effort on our part to escape the freedom we have already been given in Christ.[8]

Willis's sense that he must introduce God into the picture underscores the crucial shortcoming of psychological perspectives that view petition as little more than autosuggestion. Such proposals fail to take into account the central aspect of the working of prayer evident in the Bible — namely, that God responds directly to our petitions. For this reason, such understandings of prayer run the risk of buying into a purely naturalistic view of the universe, which leaves no room for any conception of divine intervention. As a result, the human story comes to be reduced to a closed continuum of cause and effect, in which God not only does not work but in fact cannot work in response to our heartfelt cry for the kingdom.

Having voiced this reservation, I would quickly add that exploring the psychology of prayer is not completely wrongheaded. If such explorations are not pursued in a manner that categorically denies the possibility of the in-breaking of the kingdom into our world, they can provide helpful insight into some aspects of the working of prayer. Psychological considerations can illumine how our prayer often taps

---

7. Willis, *Daring Prayer* (Atlanta: John Knox, 1977), pp. 120-21.

8. Willis, *Daring Prayer,* pp. 124-25. For a similar account, see Simpson, *The Interpretation of Prayer in the Early Church,* pp. 170-71.

into God's power and willingness to act on our behalf. God *does* work inner healing in us through our petitionary prayer. Prayer *can* lead to a "calmness and relaxation of spirit," to use the words of Gabriel Daly, as Christians in prayer learn how to face their deepest fears "by naming them in the presence of God."[9]

In the same way, God often uses intercessors as channels for healing in the lives of others. As Don Saliers rightly notes, "Prayer forms in us the disposition of compassion toward others. . . . The brokenness of the world is the arena in which we are called by love to practice costly compassion. This is the pattern laid down in the life of the one who teaches us to pray."[10] In short, understanding how prayer can involve autosuggestion emphasizes the biblical truth that we are often partners with God in the answering of prayer.

The realization that the older psychological idea of autosuggestion has its shortcomings has produced a growing interest in proposing psychological accounts of prayer that give some place to God. D. Z. Phillips offers an illuminating example. Phillips claims that understanding petition requires that we take account of the relationship to God within which the petition is voiced.

> When deep religious believers pray *for* something, they are not so much asking God to bring this about, but in a way telling him of the strength of their desires. They realize that things may not go as they wish, but they are asking to be able to go on living whatever happens.[11]

Yet in the end, Phillips does not stray far from the typical psychological understanding of prayer. He then adds, "In prayers of petition, the believer is trying to find a meaning and a hope that will deliver him from the elements in his life which threaten to destroy it," namely, "his desires."[12]

Perhaps a more promising proposal comes from Donald Capps, who draws from the psychology of communication. For him, the key

9. Daly, *Asking the Father* (Wilmington, Del.: Michael Glazier, 1982), p. 72.

10. Saliers, *The Soul in Paraphrase* (New York: Seabury Press, 1980), p. 72.

11. Phillips, *The Concept of Prayer,* Blackwell ed. (1965; Oxford: Basil Blackwell, 1981), p. 121.

12. Phillips, *The Concept of Prayer,* p. 121.

question is, Does God hear and respond? Capps is convinced that God does indeed respond. But the manner in which Capps describes this response differs radically from what most believers are in fact envisioning when they pray: "We may anticipate how God responds to a need or problem of ours, and this anticipation itself completes the dialogical circle. The petitioner somehow 'knows' how God views the matter, and this knowledge or awareness is itself an 'answer' to prayer."[13]

Despite its obvious potential in bringing God back into the loop, Capps's proposal remains inadequate as an explanation of the effects of prayer. This is not surprising, of course, for by its very nature, psychology is unable to offer a satisfying account of petitionary prayer. As a human science, its focus is too narrow. Its subject matter is limited to the human person, or even more narrowly, the human psyche. Prayer, in contrast, is conversation with God. In prayer, we voice our plea that God break into our world with his gift of the kingdom. And this cry for the kingdom releases God's willingness and power to do so. If this is what Christian prayer is, then any attempt to understand how it "works" must include God within its purview. But truly giving place to God in our understanding of prayer requires that we look at petition from a theological perspective.

Prayer and Christian Theology

By its very nature, prayer is a theological act. It is the cry *to God* for the kingdom. It is the voicing of our petitions, which ultimately are all related to the in-breaking of the reign of God to meet the needs of the present. Because petition assumes the willingness and power of God to act, any understanding of the working of prayer must appeal to the reality of God.

1. Prayer from Ritschl to Barth

Throughout the history of the church, theologians have risen to the challenge of giving an account of how prayer works. Many contempo-

13. Capps, "The Psychology of Petitionary Prayer," *Theology Today* 39, no. 2 (1982): 137.

rary proposals have arisen either as extensions of or reactions to the basic perspective that came to the fore in German liberal Protestantism in the nineteenth century.

The great liberal theologians generally drew from the idea of prayer as communion with God.[14] Albrecht Ritschl, for example, spoke of prayer as an expression of faith and humility. For him, prayer is the means of clarifying and reinforcing the basic response of the Christian to God in the face of the hindrances of life. At the heart of his proposal was the idea that prayer is to be an expression of thanksgiving and joy to the reconciling, caring God. As a consequence, Ritschl subsumed petition under thanksgiving, which he viewed as the more general form of prayer. Even in petition, he asserted, thanksgiving is to be elevated.

Wilhelm Herrmann articulated a similar understanding. In his estimation, prayer is the response of the believer to God's initiative. It is an offering of thanksgiving to the God whose love precedes human response. Prayer, then, is an expression of turning toward God and of communion with God. Like Ritschl, Herrmann subsumed petitionary prayer under thanksgiving. He viewed petition as the request for the removal of the distress of life from one's view of God. In this way, prayer becomes the application of faith to a particular circumstance of life. The purpose of petition is to bring the believer to stand in faith before the God whose help is certain.

The twentieth century occasioned the rediscovery of petitionary prayer. Prominent in this process was the work of Karl Barth. He has been so important, in fact, that Perry LeFevre has declared, "No theologian in the twentieth century has written as much about prayer as Karl Barth, and none has made it as decisive a theme either in theology or for the life of the Christian community as has Barth."[15] Similarly, George S. Hendry declared that he knew of no Protestant theologian of modern times "who has given more serious attention to prayer" than Karl Barth.[16]

Barth understood prayer as constituting — together with faith and obedience — the divinely commanded response to God's action in

---

14. For a study of this era, see Perry LeFevre, *Understandings of Prayer* (Philadelphia: Westminster, 1981), pp. 9-26.

15. LeFevre, *Understandings of Prayer,* p. 28.

16. Hendry, "The Life Line of Theology," *Princeton Seminary Bulletin* 65, no. 2 (1972): 27.

Christ. Barth viewed prayer primarily as petition, which he understood as a going toward God, an asking God to give the petitioner what he or she lacks.[17] In Barth's estimation, Christian prayer is marked decisively by petition, because this form of prayer discloses our true situation. Petition reminds us that God is the source of all good, and that as human beings we are utterly dependent and stand in need of everything.

Barth reversed the nineteenth-century ordering of the relationship between petition and thanksgiving. For him, petition forms the basis for the other aspects of prayer. Thanksgiving, in turn, arises out of the need to ask and receive of God. And confession is itself a specific petition, the request for forgiveness based on a sense of need.

In Barth's view, petition carries the assurance of not being offered in vain. God hears and responds; God alters his intentions. And because God has already given the answer to all human petitions — Christ Jesus — there are no set limits to the content of prayer.

Barth elevated the Lord's Prayer as the model for Christian praying. He declared that this prayer entails the petition that the pray-er participate in the cause of God, and that God in turn participate in the cause of God's people. And God does so, Barth added, by responding to the basic needs shared by all human beings.

George Hendry has likewise emphasized the importance of petition. In his estimation, prayer is foremost the act of the community of God's people. Petition lies at the heart of prayer, because the kingdom of God must be sought not only by faith and obedience but also by prayer, which includes petition for our human needs. For Hendry, the language of prayer is ultimately that of crying — a cry that comes after, and goes beyond, all talk.

2. A Theological Account of Petition

Theologians such as Barth and Hendry have done the church a great service in elevating petition to the very heart of Christian prayer. In so doing, they have provided helpful theological insights into the nature of prayer. Their work indicates that in contrast to purely psychological

17. This theme has been developed recently in Theodore Jennings, *Life as Worship: Prayer and Praise in Jesus' Name* (Grand Rapids: Eerdmans, 1982), esp. pp. 26-30.

engagements, a theological account of petition need not be embarrassed by the idea that God is the one to whom prayer is ultimately addressed.[18]

Two crucial assumptions about God and the world lie behind a theological conception of petition that finds its impulse in the legacy of Barth and Hendry. The first is the belief that a transcendent God can and does work in the world. This means that the universe is not a closed continuum of natural cause-and-effect shut off from the inbreaking of God. The second assumption is the belief that petition somehow elicits a response from the God who is able and willing to act in the world. The petitions of God's people are not simply directed to themselves, therefore, but come to the ear of God.

The practice of petition arises out of these two beliefs. Yet, when taken together, the two raise the central question that a helpful theological account of prayer must address: *How* do our petitions elicit God's response? How does the cry for the kingdom occasion the inbreaking of the kingdom?

Our starting point in responding to this question must lie in a particular understanding of petition. Let me state it in this manner: Petition is the laying hold of and the releasing of God's willingness and ability to act in accordance with God's will and purpose on behalf of creation, which God loves. This means that petition is not "the attempt of human importunity to overcome divine reluctance," to cite the words of E. G. Knapp-Fisher.[19] Rather, as John Bunyan said, petition is "a sincere, affectionate pouring out of the heart or soul to God, through Christ, in the strength and assistance of the Holy Spirit, for such things as God has promised, or according to his Word, for the good of the church, with submission in faith to the will of God."[20]

Several phrases in the description that I offered in the previous paragraph require further elaboration. To say that "petition is the laying hold of" is to declare that by means of prayer the pray-er taps into

18. Hendry, "The Lifeline of Theology," p. 25. For an extended discussion of the relationship between prayer and theology, see Saliers, *The Soul in Paraphrase,* pp. 82-86. See also Bernard Häring, *Prayer: The Integration of Faith and Life* (Notre Dame, Ind.: Fides Publishers, 1975), p. xi.

19. Knapp-Fisher, *Belief and Prayer* (London: Darton, Longman & Todd, 1964), p. x.

20. Bunyan, *A Discourse Touching Prayer* (1662; London: Banner of Truth Trust, 1965), p. 13.

the power and willingness of God. Prayer occasions something being released from God. This "something" is twofold — "God's willingness" and "God's ability." In making this claim, I am presupposing a specific understanding of God's nature. I am assuming that God is both willing and able to act on behalf of creation. I am declaring that God is loving in disposition and sovereign or omnipotent in power. God is both predisposed toward wanting what is good for us and able to meet any situation that we might face.

Many Christians would acknowledge that in the crucible of life it is not always easy to believe that God is both loving and all-powerful. Life situations tempt us to doubt either God's willingness (love) or God's ability (omnipotence). Prayer then becomes the struggle to accept these two aspects of what we confess to be true about God. The goal of prayer becomes that of bringing the pray-er to the point of genuine faith. When prayer has done its work, we come to trust anew this loving, powerful God.

If this is the case, then petition could be seen as an expression of our realization that we are dependent on God. Indeed, there is a close relationship between God's action and our realization of dependence. Often God will not act until we realize that we cannot make it on our own. God will not do what God desires to do until we come to see that we desperately need God's intervention in our lives. As long as we erroneously think that we can handle life's situations on our own, God simply stands aside. Divine resources do not break into our situation until we admit that life has grown too immense for our own abilities.

This idea has gained a hearing even among philosophers of religion. In a manner somewhat similar to that of D. Z. Phillips, Vincent Brümmer has explored the relational significance of prayer. Brümmer rejects the idea that prayer is intended either to inform God of what he does not know or to remind oneself of what one tends to forget. Rather, in prayer, the petitioner "*acknowledges* his personal dependence on God in a way which enables God to give him what he could not have given without the acknowledgment."[21]

Yet, as humans we often recoil at the idea that we are not self-sufficient. Petitionary prayer, therefore, is in part the struggle to admit

---

21. Brümmer, *What Are We Doing When We Pray? A Philosophical Inquiry* (London: SCM, 1984), p. 46.

our dependence. It is the struggle to overcome our human blindness and pride. It is the struggle to realize and acknowledge our deep need. And this acknowledgment is precisely what lays hold of and releases God's resources. O. Hallesby reminds us that prayer is not intended to make God generous. Rather, the struggle of prayer has as its purpose "to induce us to open our hearts to receive all that Jesus is willing to give."[22] In short, prayer is a crying to God for help, based on an awareness of dependence on God. It is the cry for the kingdom voiced by persons who realize that only the in-breaking of God's reign can remedy the challenging situations that we face. E. M. Bounds aptly comments,

> Prayer is the language of a man burdened with a sense of need. It is the voice of a beggar, conscious of his poverty, asking of another the things he needs. . . . Not to pray is not only to declare that there is nothing needed, but to admit to a nonrealization of that need.[23]

Viewed in this light, prayer resembles faith. Like faith, petition is merely opening our empty hand so that we might receive God's provision. But we must take this connection a step further. Prayer not only expresses the dependence connected to faith; it is also a declaration that we do indeed believe that God is both willing and able to act. This suggests that a significant relationship also exists between God's action and human faith. The New Testament repeatedly reminds us that God will not act unless human beings believe that God can do so. Or, to state the point in another way, the New Testament declares that faith brings results (e.g., James 1:6-8; Luke 7:50; Matt. 9:29; 13:58; 17:20; 21:21). And one meaningful expression of faith in God is petitionary prayer.

Yet we have not yet engaged the central question that I posed in this section: If petition releases God's willingness and ability to act, what does this say about God's relationship to the world? Many contemporary Christians are no longer convinced that we should picture God in heaven passively waiting for the opportunity to intervene in the world in response to human prayer.[24] Equally difficult to affirm is the seem-

---

22. Hallesby, *Prayer* (Minneapolis: Augsburg, 1931), p. 166. This same point is made by Fosdick, *The Meaning of Prayer*, pp. 62-63.

23. Bounds, *The Weapon of Prayer* (Chicago: Moody Press, 1980), p. 106.

24. Daly, *Asking the Father* (Wilmington, Del.: Michael Glazier, 1982), pp. 54-55.

ingly opposite understanding of prayer that presupposes an immutable God whose fixed plan is completely unaffected and undeterred by human petition. Maurice Nedoncelle notes the manner in which this latter outlook was prevalent among theologians in the patristic era and the Middle Ages:

> St. Thomas Aquinas, in his *Summa Theologica,* follows Origen, and maintains that prayer in no way involves a denial of the divine changelessness, for God's mind does not change and is not affected by any outside influence. We do not pray with the idea that we are going to alter what God has decided to perform; we pray in order that we may obtain what he has decided shall come about precisely through our prayers.[25]

The conclusions of the previous chapter suggest that a helpful point of departure in understanding prayer lies in its orientation to the future. Prayer, I declared, is an eschatological activity. It is directed toward the kingdom of God. In prayer, we beseech the God of the future with the request that the marks of God's rule (forgiveness, sustenance, deliverance, and the Spirit's fullness) break into our present situation, which is filled with want, need, and insufficiency. Petitionary prayer, in other words, requests the coming of the future into the present.

This eschatological orientation offers an understanding of how God can be said to be sovereign and omnipotent. God exercises sovereign rulership over creation from the vantage point of the future consummation of God's work in the history of the universe. The kingdom of God — that perfect order in which God's will is fully present — is coming, the Bible asserts. Insofar as history is moving toward that great day, and insofar as that day will come in its fullness, God is not only sovereign over the future but also sovereign over the present.

In a similar way, God is omnipotent. This term does not refer to God's supposed ability to do absolutely anything conceivable. Rather, God is omnipotent in that evil is no match for divine power. Omnipotence, therefore, speaks about God's ability and intent to overrule evil for good.

The Bible declares that God's ultimate "no" to evil is yet future. It

---

25. Nedoncelle, *The Nature and Use of Prayer* (London: Burns & Oates, 1964), p. 114.

will be spoken at the climax of history when the kingdom is fully here. God's omnipotence will be fully demonstrated at Christ's glorious return, when evil is totally banished from God's creation. But even en route to that event, evil is partially overruled in the situations of life. Paul reflected this perspective when he penned those great words that have been a source of strength to so many Christians throughout the ages: "And we know that in all things God works for the good of those who love him" (Rom. 8:28). A foretaste of God's future demonstration of rulership over evil can be experienced in every present situation. God desires to work in the present, combating the evil, sin, and fallenness that characterizes this age. And because God is able and willing to do so, he is omnipotent.

With this understanding of God's sovereignty and omnipotence in view, we are finally in a position to inquire into the nature of prayer and its role in God's program. As I have reiterated in these paragraphs, prayer is an eschatological activity. It is oriented toward the kingdom of God. In fact, each of the four aspects of prayer in the ACTS acrostic is directed toward the in-breaking of God's reign. Adoration is the celebration of the greatness of the sovereign, omnipotent God. Confession is the acknowledgment of the fallenness and incompleteness of present earthly existence, an acknowledgment that leads to a request for personal and communal forgiveness. Thanksgiving is the celebration of past experiences of the in-breaking of God's love and power into this fallen age. It is the offering of gratitude for the experiences of kingdom power that have already occurred. Petition, in turn, is the request for the in-breaking of kingdom power in the present situation. But it includes as well the cry for the coming of God's rule in its fullness, which is nothing less than the glorious appearing of our Lord and Savior Jesus Christ.

Because of its connection to the coming of the kingdom, prayer brings results. As we pray, we are able to perceive the presence of the kingdom in all areas of life. As we pray, we become the instruments of the Spirit in opening the situations we face to receive the in-breaking of God's rule in the present. And through prayer, we move history toward that day when the kingdom will arrive in its fullness and God's work in the world will reach its final goal.

This understanding of the working of prayer is grounded in a specific outlook toward the nature of reality. Ultimately, prayer's effectiveness is an outworking of God's own sovereign decision regarding the coming to be of his program in the world. En route to the return of Christ, which will mark God's final and highest assertion of sovereign rulership over the universe, God has seen fit to involve us in the enactment of the divine program. Of course, God exercises providential care, ordering the actions of humankind to serve the purposes of his plan. But at the same time, God invites human beings to participate in the coming to pass of God's program.[26]

The Bible repeatedly emphasizes the role of human action in effecting God's purposes. For example, the death of Jesus came about by the actions of human beings who sought to oppose God's will. Yet these actions served to further God's plan (Acts 2:23). And even now the stage for the return of Christ is being set by many events, including the decisions of world leaders. The interaction of human and divine agency is likewise crucial in the evangelization of the world. God's will is that the gospel be proclaimed throughout the world, but human beings are invited to become involved in the completion of this goal (Matt. 24:14; 2 Pet. 3:11-12).

So also with prayer. God wants to act in the world. But in certain areas God has decided not to act apart from prayer. Or, to restate the point positively, God has decided that the needed divine action will come only in response to prayer. In this sense, O. Hallesby was surely correct when he wrote, "God has voluntarily made Himself dependent upon our prayers."[27]

This is evident in God's decision regarding personal salvation. God offers reconciliation to all; yet God's actual saving action comes only in response to prayer (2 Pet. 3:9; Rom. 10:13). Similarly, God wants to send revival, but revival comes only in response to prayer (e.g., 2 Chron. 7:14). God's help is promised in times of trouble, but often God's assistance is experienced only because of prayer.

Norman Pittenger put it well when he wrote,

> Prayer, in the Christian sense, presupposes a creation in which human activities, like every other event or occurrence, have conse-

---

26. See Kornelis H. Miskotte, *The Roads of Prayer,* trans. John W. Doberstein (New York: Sheed & Ward, 1968), pp. 63-64. For a somewhat more strongly Calvinistic orientation, which bases prayer on God's ordaining of both ends and means, see Wayne R. Spear, *The Theology of Prayer* (Grand Rapids: Baker, 1979), p. 69.

27. Hallesby, *Prayer,* p. 167.

quences and make a difference. It assumes a world in which God is no absentee ruler but a present agent working "in, through, and under" created agencies — to use a Lutheran phrase originally referring to Christ's presence in the Lord's Supper and the material elements of bread and wine.[28]

A similar view is expressed by David Willis:

> The act of praying is free participation in the process of creation. God wills his creation into existence and elicits free participation, which his own self-limitation makes room for. The creative process is enriched, moved further toward its culmination when part of creation itself expands its consciousness of what it means to be created in the maker's image and to be freely obedient to him. God actually accommodates his purposes to include our acts.[29]

For us to be effective partners with God in the creative process requires that our minds and hearts be attuned to the divine program. It requires that we catch the vision of the glorious future that awaits humankind and all creation in the kingdom of God. One necessary means to this end is prayer. In prayer, we rebel against the status quo, to use the phrase of David F. Wells.[30] Petitionary prayer is a cry that God's kingdom come, so that all that opposes or runs contrary to the divine will may be overturned.

By means of prayer, we sift through the evil and dislocation of the present so that we might determine what must be altered if the rule of God is to be made manifest. Thereby, petition becomes the expression of a holy discontent with the present, an unwillingness to leave things as they are. In this way, even our own outlook can be transformed by means of prayer. This transformation, in turn, affects how we act in the world.[31]

God invites humans to become partners in the divine program by

28. Pittenger, *Praying Today* (Grand Rapids: Eerdmans, 1974), pp. 24-27.

29. Willis, *Daring Prayer,* pp. 126-29.

30. Wells, "Prayer: Rebelling Against the Status Quo," *Christianity Today,* November 1979, pp. 32-34.

31. Cf. LeFevre, *Radical Prayer: Contemporary Interpretations* (Chicago: Exploration Press, 1982), p. 86.

working, by evangelizing, by being Christians in the world — and also by praying. In this way, God gives the kingdom to the world. The great missionary statesman E. Stanley Jones understood this principle. He wrote,

> For in prayer you align yourself to the purposes and power of God, and He is able to do through you that He couldn't otherwise do. For this is an open universe, where some things are left open, contingent upon our doing them. If we do not do them, they will never be done. So God has left certain things open to prayer — things which will never be done except we pray.[32]

Understood in this sense, Albert Belden's remark is profound: "The Christian at last prays *with* God and not merely *to* Him."[33]

According to the Bible, then, prayer brings results. Prayer works in this way because God has decided to include humans in the divine program for the world. When we, through prayer, acknowledge our dependence on and express our faith in the loving, powerful One, our vision is redirected. Then we are able to lay hold of God's willingness and power to act on our behalf and on behalf of the entire world. As we cry for the kingdom, God's glorious rule breaks into our present. And one day, in response to our prayers, that rule will come in its fullness.

On the activity of petitioning the in-breaking of the kingdom, God places one stipulation: To be effective, prayer must be offered in accordance with God's will. What it means to pray according to the will of God is the topic of the next two chapters.

---

32. Jones, *The Way to Power and Poise* (Nashville: Abingdon-Cokesbury Press, 1949), p. 325. For an interesting discussion of the relationship between work and prayer, see C. S. Lewis, "Work and Prayer," in *God in the Dock* (Grand Rapids: Eerdmans, 1973), pp. 105-7.

33. Belden, *The Practice of Prayer* (New York: Harper & Brothers, n.d.), p. 95.

3. *What Praying according to God's Will Means*

Prayer is the cry for the kingdom. In prayer, we address the God who is willing and able to act. We petition God that the power of the future might break into the brokenness of the present. In this sense, to pray is to express our longing that the will of God be done on earth, as it is in heaven. When we pray in this manner, we actually lay hold of and release God's willingness and ability to act in accordance with the divine will on behalf of the creation that God loves. No wonder the early Christians were so confident in the power of prayer! John encapsulates the attitude of the apostolic church in these words: "This is the assurance that we have in approaching God: that if we ask anything according to his will, he hears us. And if we know that he hears us — whatever we ask — we know that we have what we asked of him" (1 John 5:14-15).

In this short statement, the apostle declares that Christians can enjoy the same certainty in approaching God that Jesus knew. Yet, rather than offering a blanket promise for us to claim and potentially abuse, John carefully voices a crucial stipulation: "if we ask anything according to his will." This little conditional clause raises a huge question: What determines whether or not a prayer is according to God's will?

The goal of this chapter and the next is to engage this important matter. To this end, in this chapter I develop the principles of such prayer, and then in the next chapter I look at their practical outworking. My conviction, which I unpack in the following paragraphs, is that "praying according to God's will" has to do with both the petitioner and the petition.

The Characteristics of the Petitioner

When we hear that prayer must be offered in accordance with God's will, our initial response might be to assume that the crucial aspect has to do with what we ask for. To focus first on our petitions, however, is to put the cart before the horse. Rather than what we say, our first concern ought to be who we are. Two people can voice to God the very same petition; yet one prayer ends up being in accordance with God's will, whereas the other does not. What makes the difference in this situation is not the petition itself, for the requests are identical. The difference lies with the petitioner.

For prayer to be in accordance with God's will, several characteristics must be true of the one who is praying.

1. Spiritual Condition

The first characteristic relates to the petitioner's spiritual condition. The spiritual vitality of the one who prays determines in part whether or not prayer is according to God's will. We might formulate this into a first principle of prayer: Spirituality leads to effective praying, whereas the prayer of the unspiritual person is of no avail.[1]

This principle lies at the heart of James's instructions for praying for the sick, which I cited in Chapter Two (James 5:14-15). The importance of personal spirituality in petition is evident in James's declaration that the sick person should call the elders. Because the elders were the leaders in the early church, they were to be people who walked in the Spirit. What James offers implicitly in this guideline he then states explicitly in the next verse: "The prayer of a righteous person is powerful and effective" (v. 16, NIV ILE). And just to make sure that we get the point, he then illustrates the principle from the Old Testament. The story of Elijah indicates how a righteous prophet of God was able to work great feats through prayer.

Lack of spirituality, in contrast, leads to ineffective praying. Sin, the Bible repeatedly declares, hinders prayer.[2] For example, the psalmist ac-

---

1. For a discussion of twelve problems that lead to unanswered prayer, see John Allan Lavender, *Why Prayers Are Unanswered* (Valley Forge, Pa.: Judson Press, 1967).

2. See R. A. Torrey, *How to Pray* (Chicago: Moody Press, n.d.), pp. 74ff. See also

knowledges, "If I had cherished sin in my heart, the Lord would not have listened" (Ps. 66:18). Hence, if the Holy Spirit has pointed out the presence of sin in my life, I must confess and forsake the sin for my prayer to be effective. Cherishing that sin, refusing to let go of it, will prevent the Lord from giving attention to my prayer.

A second example comes from the lips of our Lord: "And when you stand praying, if you hold anything against anyone, forgive them, so that the Father in heaven may forgive your sins" (Mark 11:25, NIV ILE). According to Jesus, an unforgiving spirit hinders prayer. For this reason the Lord's Prayer adds, "Forgive us our debts, as we also have forgiven our debtors" (Matt. 6:12).

Third, interpersonal problems hinder prayer. Jesus said, "Therefore, if you are offering your gift at the altar and there remember that your brother or sister has something against you, leave your gift in front of the altar. First go and be reconciled to them; then come and offer your gift" (Matt. 5:23-24, NIV ILE). Sacrifices in the Jewish economy were to be accompanied by prayer. In these words in his Sermon on the Mount, Jesus describes a situation in which the one praying has previously committed some offense against another. He instructs the offending party to seek out the injured person and notes that reconciliation between them is crucial for effectiveness in prayer.

In his first epistle, Peter provides a fourth example: "Husbands, in the same way be considerate as you live with your wives, and treat them with respect as the weaker partner and as heirs with you of the gracious gift of life, so that nothing will hinder your prayers" (1 Pet. 3:7). Marital relationships, Peter declares, can affect one's prayer life. James Houston, quoting another author, states it well: "The sighs of the injured wife come between the husband's prayers and God's hearing."[3] Problems in the family must be rooted out if prayer is to be unhindered.

A fifth example is found in the book of Proverbs: "If you shut your ears to the cry of the poor, you too will cry out and not be answered" (Prov. 21:13, NIV ILE). We repeatedly cry out to God in the midst of life's trials. However, if we are hardened to the cries of others — if we are

---

J. Oswald Sanders, *Prayer Power Unlimited* (Minneapolis: World Wide Publications, 1977), pp. 78-85.

3. Houston, *The Transforming Power of Prayer: Deepening Your Friendship with God* (Colorado Springs: NavPress, 1996), p. 150.

stingy and unwilling to help those around us who are in need — then our own cries to God will not be heard.

The understanding of prayer that I developed in Chapter Two offers insight into why our spiritual condition and effective prayer are so closely related. I described petition as the laying hold of God's willingness and ability to act in accordance with the divine will. Prayer is the cry for the kingdom. To pray is to say to God, "Your will be done on earth as it is in heaven." The New Testament draws a connection between voicing this kind of prayer and personal spirituality. According to the writers of Scripture, the spiritual person is being led by the Spirit of God.[4] This, in turn, results in the spiritual Christian being in fellowship with God and growing in the knowledge of God's character, ways, and will. When we are taught by the Spirit in this manner, Spirit-led prayer naturally follows.[5] Our prayer comes to reflect God's will because it is in fact the Spirit within us who moves us to pray. And the Spirit, who knows the mind of God, prompts us to pray in accordance with God's mind. Such Spirit-filled prayer releases the willingness of God to act, because such prayer is indeed in accordance with God's plan. The Spirit-filled pray-er is enlightened by the Spirit to request what would truly mark the in-breaking of the kingdom into the present situation.

The unspiritual person, in contrast, cannot lay hold of God's willingness to act. God will not respond when the petitioner is harboring unconfessed sin. As Isaiah observed, "Surely the arm of the LORD is not too short to save, nor his ear too dull to hear. But your iniquities have separated you from your God; your sins have hidden his face from you, so that he will not hear" (Isa. 59:1-2; see also Jer. 5:25). The type of prayer that God desires from the person living in sin is not petition but confession.[6]

We can gain a sense as to why this is the case by looking again at the ACTS acrostic. This device is not merely a way of helping us remember

4. The role of the Spirit in prayer is discussed by Andrew Murray in *With Christ in the School of Prayer* (Old Tappan, N.J.: Revell, 1953), pp. 139-44. See also Wayne R. Spear, *The Theology of Prayer* (Grand Rapids: Baker, 1979), pp. 42-47.

5. For a discussion of the characteristics of prayer in the Spirit, see R. A. Torrey, *The Power of Prayer* (Grand Rapids: Zondervan, 1955), pp. 178-88.

6. See Perry LeFevre, *Radical Prayer: Contemporary Interpretations* (Chicago: Exploration Press, 1982), p. 87.

the four parts of the complete prayer life. Rather, it embodies the proper order that prayer is to follow. Petition (supplication) comes last because it is the outworking of a thankful heart that has come to know the forgiveness of an awe-inspiring God. The person who seeks to engage in supplication while bypassing confession is attempting to circumvent this progression. In short, unspiritual Christians fail to pray in accordance with God's will because they refuse to place confession before petition.

2. Motivation

The second crucial characteristic of the one who would pray in accordance with God's will is motivation. The motivation behind prayer determines whether or not a petition is offered according to God's will. Thus, a second principle of prayer is this: Godly motivation brings results, whereas improper motivation leads to ineffectiveness.

Of course, godly concerns ought to motivate all that we do. Paul declared quite forthrightly, "So whether you eat or drink or whatever you do, do it all for the glory of God" (1 Cor. 10:31). Among the concerns that comprise godly motivation, none is more crucial than the desire that God be glorified — that God's name be honored, that God's reputation be enhanced in the world. The concern for God's glory ought to be a compelling motivation in every aspect of a Christian's life. O. Hallesby comments,

> If we make use of prayer, not to wrest from God advantages for ourselves or our dear ones, or to escape from tribulations and difficulties, but to call down upon ourselves and others those things which will glorify the name of God, then we shall see the strongest and boldest promises of the Bible about prayer fulfilled also in our weak, little prayer life.[7]

Related to this is the concern for the growth of the kingdom of God. Actually, these two desires lie at the heart of the Lord's Prayer. The first petition, "Our Father in heaven, hallowed be your name," mirrors

7. Hallesby, *Prayer* (Minneapolis: Augsburg, 1931), p. 138.

concern for God's glory. The second, "your kingdom come, your will be done on earth as it is in heaven," expresses the concern that God's reign be advanced on earth. These two considerations ought to form the foundational motivation not only for Christian life but also for Christian prayer. Our calling as disciples of Jesus is to engage in the business of the King. Our awareness of this ought to shape our prayer. Each petition that we voice to God should be offered with a fervent desire that God be glorified and God's kingdom expanded.

Godly motivation also includes concern for the welfare of others. This is the specific business of the King in the world. God desires that human beings reach their full, divinely given potential. God is concerned that all share in the good things of the earth and enjoy abundant life. Paul's prayers reflect this kind of concern. The apostle was continually interested in the spiritual growth of his recipients. His central desire was that they come to a full knowledge of — that is, that they experience fully — the love of Christ. This same concern ought to motivate our praying as well.

Improper motivation, in contrast, brings negative results. Such motivation can lead God to deny our requests. James says, "When you ask, you do not receive, because you ask with wrong motives, that you may spend what you get on your pleasures" (James 4:3). Often our petitions are motivated by selfishness. We ask God to bestow good things on us, but our actual intent is to squander God's gifts.

Improper motivation can also result in God granting our requests, but with dire consequences. In tempting Jesus, Satan sought to bring our Lord to use his power with God in an improper manner. This is especially evident in the second temptation as recorded in Matthew's Gospel:

> Then the devil took him to the holy city and had him stand on the highest point of the temple. "If you are the Son of God," he said, "throw yourself down. For it is written: 'He will command his angels concerning you, and they will lift you up in their hands, so that you will not strike your foot against a stone.'" Jesus answered him, "It is also written: 'Do not put the Lord your God to the test.'" (Matt. 4:5-6)

Such a display of prayer power would have trivialized the Father's promise to protect the Son. And it would have been a detriment to the fulfillment of Jesus' mission.

An incident in the history of ancient Israel offers another example. While the Israelites wandered in the wilderness, God provided them with food to eat each day. However, they were not satisfied with God's provision:

> The rabble with them began to crave other food, and again the Israelites started wailing and said, "If only we had meat to eat! We remember the fish we ate in Egypt at no cost — also the cucumbers, melons, leeks, onions and garlic. But now we have lost our appetite; we never see anything but this manna!" (Num. 11:4-6)

In response, God decided to show the negative consequences of this improperly motivated petition:

> Tell the people: "Consecrate yourselves in preparation for tomorrow, when you will eat meat. The LORD heard you when you wailed, 'If only we had meat to eat! We were better off in Egypt!' Now the LORD will give you meat, and you will eat it. You will not eat it for just one day, or two days, or five, ten or twenty days, but for a whole month — until it comes out of your nostrils and you loathe it — because you have rejected the LORD, who is among you, and have wailed before him, saying, 'Why did we ever leave Egypt?'" (Num. 11:18-20).

Consider as well the story of Balaam (Num. 22). Balak, the king of the Moabites, approached this prophet to curse Israel. Balaam repeatedly petitioned God regarding the matter, and each time God warned Balaam not to go with the Moabite king. But the prophet desperately wanted to do Balak's bidding. So in the end God gave him permission to do so. But Balaam discovered, to his regret, that this led to his undoing (Num. 31:8). The book of Revelation pronounces the final biblical judgment on him, for it characterizes Balaam as the one "who taught Balak to entice the Israelites to sin" (Rev. 2:14). No wonder the personal testimony of many Christians is "I have lived long enough to become grateful that God has not answered all my requests."

Proper motivation is significant for prayer offered in accordance with God's will. Yet it is not always easy for us to follow this principle. At times, we claim that we are concerned for God's glory, God's kingdom, and the welfare of others, but in fact our motivation is pure selfishness.

When this occurs, prayer becomes hypocritical. We might continue to follow the proper prayer routine and even speak the right words. Nevertheless, the motivation that drives us to pray is not the desire that God's rule be present in the here and now. In such prayers we give only lip service to petitioning that the kingdom break into the present.

3. Cooperation

A third crucial characteristic of the petitioner is cooperation. The presence or absence of a spirit of cooperation determines whether or not prayer is offered in accordance with God's will. This leads to a third principle of prayer: The willingness to cooperate with God in the granting of one's request brings results, whereas unwillingness to be God's tool leads to ineffectiveness.

The prayer that is according to God's will is the one in which we place everything that we have and are at God's disposal in bringing about the answer to our request. A petition accompanied by an unwillingness to become involved, in contrast, evidences a lack of genuine concern for the situation. Kornelis H. Miskotte observes,

> Much of the yammering about the inertia of history, much of the grieving over failure of the Lord to come again, much of the problematizing that only lets the bitterness of life and fate have the best of it, many laments about the silence of God which sends back our prayers unheard are not genuine, because we have not really believed that concrete prayer quite directly includes concrete action. We may therefore also confidently assume that much prayerlessness is a reaction from "well-meant" Christian prayers which were not really well-meant at all.[8]

The importance of a willingness to cooperate with God in the answering of our prayers arises out of God's own nature. God does not exist to do our bidding. Nor is God's task that of accomplishing for us what we should be doing ourselves. Consider Jesus' raising of Lazarus

---

8. Miskotte, *The Roads of Prayer,* trans. John W. Doberstein (New York: Sheed & Ward, 1968), p. 62.

(John 11). When the Lord came to the tomb, he commanded the onlookers to take away the stone that had been rolled in front of the entrance (v. 38). The one who had the power to raise the dead likewise had the ability to command the stone to move away from the tomb. Yet Jesus asked the bystanders to take that action themselves. Moreover, when Lazarus came out of the tomb, his hands and feet remained bound with strips of linen, and a cloth was still wrapped around his face (v. 44). The one who could raise the dead had the power to command the bindings to fall from the resuscitated man. Yet he said to the bystanders, "Take off the grave clothes and let him go" (v. 44). Why? Jesus was not needed to perform such "miracles" as moving the stone and loosening the linen strips. These tasks could readily be done by Lazarus's friends. What Jesus *was* needed for was to do what only Jesus could do: to exercise authority over death and to restore life.

This incident is instructive for us as well. We sometimes ask God to accomplish in our midst what we in fact should be doing ourselves. Uncooperative prayer — petitioning God while being unwilling to get involved — is ultimately ineffective. Prayer must be accompanied by cooperation, by a willingness to be engaged in the process of answering our requests.

The importance of cooperation arises likewise out of the nature of God's plan in the world. As I spelled out in Chapter Two, God has ordained that we play important roles in the accomplishing of God's intentions and goals. And this includes participating in the task of answering our prayers. A grand biblical example of this aspect of God's intention is found in Matthew's Gospel. Surveying the spiritual situation in Galilee, Jesus said to the disciples, "The harvest is plentiful but the workers are few. Ask the Lord of the harvest, therefore, to send out workers into his harvest field" (Matt. 9:37-38). In the next chapter, Matthew presents Jesus giving his disciples a set of missionary instructions and sending them into the harvest field. We can readily surmise what had happened between the close of the ninth and the beginning of the tenth chapter. After hearing Jesus' call to prayer, the disciples beseeched the Lord of the harvest, only to discover that the Lord's plan was to use them to answer their request.

The same principle is applicable to us. Those who pray just might discover that they are agents of the answer. Ethel Barrett offers this story as an illustration:

There was a man once who did not believe in God. He made a great point of it. He was a scoffer loud and clear. His Christian acquaintances began to pray for him. Every time they happened to be together and there was prayer they included him in it: "Lord, save brother so and so. He is not yet a brother." But there was one man in this group who decided to go one step further. After one of these sessions he got his horse and buggy and drove to the man's house. "I just want you to know that I am concerned about you and that I have prayed for your salvation, and that I cannot bear for you to be lost," he said, and then he rode away.[9]

In short, our acts of petitioning God for the in-breaking of the kingdom should lead us to genuine soul-searching. Viewed from this perspective, prayer becomes the occasion for us to ask: What is my spiritual condition? Perhaps God is waiting for my prayer of repentance and for fruit in my life before listening to my petitions. Why do I want God to grant this request? Perhaps my motives are purely selfish; perhaps I don't really desire that God be glorified, that God's kingdom be advanced, and that the welfare of others be heightened. And am I willing to be the answer to my own petition? Perhaps I need to lay myself at God's disposal for the accomplishing of this request.

These three questions are crucial. They reveal the extent to which we are becoming the kind of petitioners whose prayers are offered in accordance with God's will.

The Characteristics of the Petition

With this view of the importance of ourselves as petitioners who come to God in prayer, we can now turn our attention to the petitions themselves. The burning question, of course, is this: How can we know whether or not our requests are in line with God's will? Ultimately, the only sure guide in this, as in every aspect of the Christian faith, is the divine revelation disclosed in Scripture.

As Christians, we naturally turn to the Bible to find God's will. The

9. Barrett, *Sometimes I Feel Like a Blob* (Glendale, Calif.: Regal Books, 1965).

Scriptures reveal the divine will in two basic ways. Certain aspects of the will of God are explicitly given in Scripture. For example, the Bible teaches that God desires that all persons come to repentance and faith (2 Pet. 3:9; 1 Tim. 2:4; cf. Ezek. 18:23), that the world be evangelized (Matt. 28:19; Acts 1:8; Matt. 24:14), and that Christians grow in Christlikeness (Eph. 4:13, 15). We find God's will through the Bible likewise as we discover principles that are applicable to the situations we encounter.

This leads to a fourth principle of prayer according to God's will: Because we come to know and understand God's will through the Bible, the kind of prayer that is in accordance with the will of God is *biblical* prayer. And biblical prayer is prayer that draws its petitions — even its very language — from Scripture. Petitions that are seasoned with glimpses of God's purposes as disclosed in Scripture, therefore, are effective, whereas praying in a manner that knows nothing of God's Word brings at best only paltry results.

An incident in the life of the early church provides an instructive biblical example of this kind of praying. Peter and John had been commanded by the officials in Jerusalem not to proclaim the message of Jesus. When the officials released the two apostles, they returned to the upper room and reported to the others what the Jewish leaders had told them. Upon hearing the threats of the rulers, the believers "raised their voices together in prayer to God" (Acts 4:23-24). Luke provides a snapshot of the content of this prayer:

> Sovereign Lord, you made the heaven and the earth and the sea, and everything in them. You spoke by the Holy Spirit through the mouth of your servant, our father David: "Why do the nations rage and the peoples plot in vain?" (vv. 24-25)

Note that the prayer began by acknowledging God's sovereignty over creation. This was followed by a quotation from the Second Psalm regarding the rebellion of the peoples of the earth against the sovereign God. The petitioners then applied the word of God as found in Psalm 2 to their present situation:

> Indeed Herod and Pontius Pilate met together with the Gentiles and the people of Israel in this city to conspire against your holy servant Je-

sus, whom you anointed. . . . Now, Lord, consider their threats and enable your servants to speak your word with great boldness. (vv. 27, 29)

In this manner, the psalm formed the basis for the petition that God grant them boldness to speak. How did God respond? Luke reports, "The place where they were meeting was shaken. And they were all filled with the Holy Spirit and spoke the word of God boldly" (v. 31).

The pattern that we find in Acts 4 has been repeated in the lives of Christians throughout church history. To cite one example: It is said that George Mueller would often sit with an open Bible, meditating on the Scriptures. Out of his devotional life grew his prayers, which gave him certainty in requesting help from God. E. M. Bounds describes Mueller's experience:

At one time his practice was to give himself to prayer after having dressed in the morning. Then his plan underwent a change. As he himself put it: "I saw the most important thing I had to do was to give myself to the reading of the Word of God, and to meditation on it. . . . I began, therefore, to meditate on the New Testament early in the morning. . . . The result I have found to be almost invariably thus, that after a very few minutes my soul has been led to confession, or to thanksgiving, or to intercession, or to supplication; so that, though I did not, as it were, give myself to prayer, but to meditation, yet it turned almost immediately more or less into prayer."[10]

Because our knowledge of God's will comes through the Scriptures, it is imperative that reading and studying the Bible become a central aspect of our lives. Such study must then be integrated into our praying. One focal point for this kind of integration of Scripture and prayer can be our time of daily personal devotions. A technique that I have found helpful in this context is to draw from the Scripture texts that I have just read in my devotions the petitions of the prayer that I then offer. By following exercises such as this, we can develop the ability to form all of our petitions on the basis of what we have come to know about God's will through the reading of God's Word.

10. Bounds, *Purpose in Prayer* (London: Marshall Brothers, n.d.), p. 53. The account of Mueller is also reprinted in Murray, *With Christ in the School of Prayer,* pp. 178-92.

Our goal ought to be to come to the point at which the Word of God is integrated into our supplications on every occasion and the Bible is drawn into every facet of our prayer life. Then, when we find ourselves burdened to bring a request to God, we can call to mind Scripture texts that offer insight into the situation at hand or promises that ought to inform our petitions in the situation. In this manner, the revealed will of God in the Bible can increasingly become the basis for the prayers that we voice to God so that our petitions increasingly come to reflect the divine will. Because God desires to act according to his revealed will and to act in response to prayer, we can be bold in petitioning the Lord of the universe to fulfill his program. We may boldly pray for the accomplishment of specific aspects of God's revealed will. As we do so, we are truly petitioning for the in-breaking of the kingdom into the present situation. We are asking that God's will be done on earth as it is in heaven.

Prayer according to God's will, then, carries two prerequisites. Through prayer the petitioner must seek to be transformed by God's Spirit into a spiritually minded, properly motivated, cooperative child of God. And as we pray, we seek to bring the requests that we offer to reflect increasingly God's own purposes and will as revealed in the Bible. When this occurs, we will be amazed at how God acts in response to our prayers and releases the power of the kingdom into the present. For as Theodore Jennings rightly noted, prayer "is simply a holding of God to his promise."[11]

11. Jennings, *Life as Worship: Prayer and Praise in Jesus' Name* (Grand Rapids: Eerdmans, 1982), p. 56.

4. How to Pray according to God's Will

Petitionary prayer is laying hold of God's willingness and ability to act in accordance with the divine will. Consequently, effective prayer is prayer that is in accordance with God's will. And praying in this manner is a function both of the petitioner and of the petition. With this basic perspective in view, I now want to look at some of the areas of life that elicit our concern. In so doing, I will seek to indicate how it is possible in practice to pray according to God's will.

The General Pattern

Ultimately, all supplication is a request for God to act. It is a cry for the kingdom. It is a request that God's rule break into the present. In short, all supplication is addressed to the One who is able and willing to bestow the kingdom as a gift of grace.

Ultimately, all the effects that are occasioned by petition come as God responds to our supplication. Prayer affects the one who prays for his or her own needs when God's power is released toward the petitioner in response to prayer. Prayer affects the one for whom intercession is offered when God's power is released in response to such intercession.[1] Prayer affects spiritual powers as God's power is released by

1. For a discussion of intercession as union of the intercessor with the divine will and energy, see Olive Wyon, *The School of Prayer* (New York: Macmillan, 1963), pp. 174-79; see also John E. Biersdorf, *Healing of Purpose* (Nashville: Abingdon, 1985), p. 185. In *Come Pray with Me* (Grand Rapids: Zondervan, 1977), Carolyn Rhea offers several metaphors to assist in understanding the working of intercession (pp. 58-63).

means of petition.[2] In each of these situations, therefore, prayer moves *God* to act.

This means that all supplication is ultimately a request for God to act. Nevertheless, only those prayers will be effective that beseech God to act according to the divine will and plan. Such prayer embodies the plea "Your kingdom come, your will be done on earth as it is in heaven." This prayer is heard by God and releases God's response. For this reason, in every circumstance our primary goal as we pray should be to discern what it would mean for the kingdom to break into the present. Then we are able to petition God accordingly. In this manner, our prayer becomes the cry for the concrete in-breaking of the kingdom into the particular situation that we face. To this end, our petitioning should draw from and be shaped by what we have come to know about God's character, God's will, and the nature of God's rule. In fact, the more we come to know about God's character, ways in the world, and plans for creation, the more dynamic our prayer life will be. Unfruitful prayer, in contrast, often has its root in our failure to comprehend spiritual truth.

One source of rich dividends in prayer is an understanding of the specific roles of each of the three persons of the Trinity. The Bible teaches that the Father is the One from whom not only the universe but also every good gift comes. The Son, in turn, is the redeemer and the revealer of God's nature. And the Holy Spirit is the divine presence in the world, the church, and each Christian, bringing the purposes of the one God to completion.

In keeping with the differentiation of roles within the triune God, generally we ought to bring our petitions to the Father as the source of provision for every need. As we do, we can link our requests for the Father's provision with biblical promises that speak of his willingness to provide for us. Our prayers for divine provision can follow this pattern: "Father, you have promised in your word that . . . [interjecting a biblical promise or truth about the nature of our heavenly Father]. On the basis of this promise, we now ask that you act according to your own nature [followed by what we sense would characterize the in-breaking of

---

2. At times a believer may in the name of Jesus address a command directly to Satan or a demon. Such action, although done in the power of the Savior, is not prayer, for by definition prayer is addressed only to God.

God's rule into this situation]. By faith we anticipate your response to our petition."

On occasion, we might deem it appropriate to address a petition to the Holy Spirit.[3] Such a prayer could be formed as follows: "Holy Spirit, you are active in the world with the task of . . . [interjecting a statement regarding the Spirit's mission]. Therefore, we ask that you minister in this situation in accordance with your nature and role, namely . . . [adding the specific request for the Spirit's action]." In this manner, we invoke the presence of the Spirit to fulfill his own mission in the world. Of course, a petition for the activity of the Spirit could also be addressed to the Father: "Father, you have sent the Spirit into the world with the task of. . . . Therefore, we invite the presence of your Spirit in this situation, to carry out the mission entrusted to him."

This kind of praying necessitates a growing acquaintance with the nature and will of God as revealed in the Bible and with the particular tasks of each of the Trinitarian persons. We do well, therefore, to search the Scriptures continually and to seek diligently to deepen our theological understanding of the mystery of the triune God. It is with this truth in view that one Christian declared, "We are often so unsuccessful in our praying because we have neglected to learn of God from the Scriptures."

Praying in Situations of Christian Concern

I believe that we can follow the general pattern of praying outlined above in every circumstance of life. In each situation, we seek to discover what the in-breaking of the kingdom would entail and then to pray accordingly. To see more specifically how this general approach can lead to more effective praying, let us consider several situations that are of special concern to us as Christians.

---

3. See *The Great Christian Doctrines,* ed. James Hastings (Edinburgh: T&T Clark, 1915), pp. 390ff.; Lehman Strauss, *Sense and Nonsense about Prayer* (Chicago: Moody, 1974), p. 121.

1. Praying for Those Who Have Not
Committed Their Lives to Christ

Christians are, of course, naturally concerned about people who are not yet within the body of Christ. Most of us could likely list several friends, colleagues, acquaintances, or relatives whom we would like to see come to the Lord. How might we most effectively intercede for them before our loving heavenly Father?

The prayer that will be heard by God is prayer that is in accordance with the divine will. Therefore, the question we must ask in this connection is, What kind of prayer is in keeping with God's will in this situation? I find in the Bible six crucial truths about people who have not yet given their lives to Christ, truths which ought to inform the manner in which we intercede for them.

First, God's will is that everyone should repent and come to the knowledge of the truth. Peter writes, "The Lord is not slow in keeping his promise, as some understand slowness. He is patient with you, not wanting anyone to perish, but everyone to come to repentance" (2 Pet. 3:9; see also 1 Tim. 2:4). Peter places this declaration within his discussion of the future day of the Lord. In this context, he notes that the reason the coming judgment has not yet arrived is that God is patient. God does not want those who have not yet repented to face eternal doom. God is patiently waiting, providing opportunity for people to come to faith. As Ezekiel noted and Jesus reiterated, God does not delight in the death of the wicked, but rejoices when a sinful person repents. God's parental heart longs for the wayward to come home.

The second truth is that God has acted in Christ on behalf of all persons. In Christ, God extends his hand of reconciliation, even though we have turned away from him. Paul succinctly articulates this truth:

All this is from God, who reconciled us to himself through Christ and gave us the ministry of reconciliation: that God was reconciling the world to himself in Christ, not counting people's sins against them. And he has committed to us the message of reconciliation. We are therefore Christ's ambassadors, as though God were making his appeal through us. We implore you on Christ's behalf: Be reconciled to God. God made him who had no sin to be sin for us, so that in him we might become the righteousness of God. (2 Cor. 5:18-21, NIV ILE)

By acting in Christ for the reconciliation of the world, God has done everything that is necessary for the salvation of everyone. This means that the difficulty that must be overcome for someone to be saved lies not with God but with the wayward person.

Third, despite Christ's reconciling work, many people choose to remain unreconciled to God. Why? Satan has blinded them so that they cannot see the truth of the gospel. Paul succinctly states this spiritual truth: "The god of this age has blinded the minds of unbelievers, so that they cannot see the light of the gospel of the glory of Christ, who is the image of God" (2 Cor. 4:4).

The activity of the Holy Spirit to counteract Satan's blinding of human beings is the fourth truth. Jesus himself announced that he would send the Spirit, who would then engage in a threefold ministry of conviction in the world:

> When he comes, he will convict the world of guilt in regard to sin and righteousness and judgment: in regard to sin, because people do not believe in me; in regard to righteousness, because I am going to the Father, where you can see me no longer; and in regard to judgment, because the prince of this world now stands condemned. (John 16:8-11, NIV ILE)

Alas, Christians are often tempted to take upon themselves the task of convincing others that they are sinners. Ultimately, however, attempting to do so is futile. The conviction of sin is the work of the Spirit. Our role is to proclaim Christ in his holiness and purity, and allow the Holy Spirit to engage in his convicting ministry.

This brings us to consider what our task in fact is. The fifth biblical truth is that we are called to proclaim the gospel. Through such proclamation, others are brought to salvation. This theme is found repeatedly in the New Testament. Paul, for example, states,

> As the Scripture says, "Anyone who trusts in him will never be put to shame." For there is no difference between Jew and Gentile — the same Lord is Lord of all and richly blesses all who call on him, for, "Everyone who calls on the name of the Lord will be saved."
>
> How, then, can they call on the one they have not believed in? And how can they believe in the one of whom they have not heard? And

how can they hear without someone preaching to them? And how can they preach unless they are sent? As it is written, "How beautiful are the feet of those who bring good news!" (Rom. 10:11-15)[4]

As we proclaim in word and act the good news of Jesus Christ, those who hear are enabled to respond to God's gracious offer of salvation.

Finally, the Bible declares that everyone who hears the good news can be saved. Salvation is possible because in his ministry Christ has defeated and bound Satan, so that Satan's captives can go free. The author of the book of Hebrews writes, "Since the children have flesh and blood, he too shared in their humanity so that by his death he might destroy him who holds the power of death — that is, the devil — and free those who all their lives were held in slavery by their fear of death" (Heb. 2:14-15).[5]

These six principles provide a basis for praying on behalf of others. God's will for those outside of Christ is that they come to salvation. God has acted in Christ on their behalf. Satan, however, blinds them. Yet the Holy Spirit has been sent to convince such persons of their sinfulness and their need for a Savior. As we proclaim the gospel, hearers are given the opportunity to be saved. All of this is possible because in his ministry Jesus has defeated Satan.

When we realize the significance of these truths, we are enabled to pray for others in faith and with hope. In prayer, we can boldly form petitions that reflect what the Bible has revealed regarding God's will, Christ's provision, and the Spirit's role in advancing the divine program. Viewed in this light, Christian prayer is not an attempt to convince God to save the lost. In Christ, God has already acted for their salvation. Rather, by applying biblical truth to this situation, we are led to direct our petitions toward the task of eliminating the impediments that hinder others from embracing the gospel. Through prayer, we release God's willingness to minister to those for whom we intercede. To this end, we form our petitions in a manner that reflects our awareness that requests which flow from God's Word are in accordance with God's will. In so doing, we invoke the in-breaking of the kingdom into the present situation.

4. See also 1 Cor. 1:21-25; 2 Cor. 5:18-20.
5. See also Luke 11:17-22.

Effective prayer for those who have not yet committed themselves to Christ requires that we become sensitive to and discerning of the spiritual condition of those for whom we pray. It is especially crucial that we gain a sense of where they stand in the process of moving toward faith. As we discern their spiritual situation, we are able to invoke the work of God in their lives at precisely the point of need. For example, if we discern that a friend is not yet aware of his or her own personal sinfulness, we can invite the Holy Spirit to engage in his convicting work in their lives. Our prayer might follow this pattern: "Father, my friend has yet to admit that her life is displeasing to you. I know from Scripture that it is the task of the Spirit to convince people of their personal sinfulness. Therefore, send the Spirit to minister in my friend's life in this way. Send situations her way that will lead her to acknowledge and then face the reality of her personal need."

If our friend has not yet heard the gospel in a manner in which he or she can understand it, we can petition the Father to send proclaimers of the word, knowing that this too is in keeping with the will of God. "Father," we can boldly pray, "the Scriptures declare that by the proclamation of the word, others are brought to salvation. My friend needs to hear the good news. Send emissaries, members of Christ's body, to speak in a way that he can understand the gospel." Of course, praying in this manner can be deemed to be "in the will of God" only if we are willing to cooperate with God in this matter. Cooperation might include our willingness to be the answer to our petition. It might require that we be willing to add, "Send me, Lord."

When distance separates us from the one for whom we are burdened, we can petition God to bring other Christians into his or her life. We can direct our petition toward the dispatching of proclaimers of the gospel in the locale in which our friend resides. Even in such cases our cooperation might be helpful. Perhaps God's Spirit would direct us to alert a church in that location to the presence of our needy friend.

As the gospel is being proclaimed, we can petition God to bless the proclaimed word in accordance with this biblical promise: "So is my word that goes out from my mouth: It will not return to me empty, but will accomplish what I desire and achieve the purpose for which I sent it" (Isa. 55:11). In each situation, our prayer might follow this form: "Father, as the gospel is proclaimed to my friend, energize it with the presence of your Spirit, in accordance with the promise given through Isaiah."[6]

Finally, through the entire process we can pray that Satan's blinding be overcome. At this point, the goal of intercession becomes that of freeing our friend's will of "the warping influences that now twist it awry," to cite S. D. Gordon's insightful characterization.[7] Because Christ has defeated Satan and thereby has made salvation possible for all, Satan's hold on human beings is illegitimate. Satan has no right to those whom he holds in captivity. This truth, too, can be directed to God in prayer: "Father, Satan has blinded the eyes of my friend so that he cannot see. Yet the devil has no right to my friend, because Christ has come in order to release Satan's captives, as stated in Hebrews 2. Now, therefore, I ask that by the power of the Holy Spirit the blinding influence of Satan be nullified, so that this captive might be set free." We might on occasion even be led by the Spirit boldly to command Satan in the name of Jesus to let go of the one he is holding under his sway.

In these various ways, our awareness of the biblical truths about salvation can lead us to bold, directed prayer for those who have not yet come to faith in Christ. In prayer, we lift our concern for them to God, drawing our petitions from Scripture in a manner that is appropriate to what we have come to learn about their spiritual condition and need. All such prayer ultimately follows a general pattern:

> Father, you know of my great concern for my friend. Just as Paul was concerned for Israel's salvation (Rom. 10:1), so also I am concerned for the salvation of my friend. I thank you that you love her even more than I do and are more concerned than I am. I know that your will is that my friend repent and be saved. It is for this reason that you sent Christ. I realize that Satan seeks to prevent my friend from responding to the gospel. Yet Christ has defeated the devil, and therefore Satan's hold can be broken. Send your Spirit to convince my friend of personal sin and to draw her attention to Christ. Send messengers to bring the good news and bless the proclamation of the

---

6. See Watchman Nee, *The Prayer Ministry of the Church* (New York: Christian Fellowship Publishers, Inc., 1973), pp. 104-7.

7. Gordon, *Quiet Talks on Prayer* (London: Fleming H. Revell Co., n.d.), pp. 192-93.

gospel as you promised to do. It is in faith that I bring this prayer to you, because I know that it is given in accordance with your will.

How much more meaningful is this kind of praying than the typical generic petition, "Lord, save my friend." Dynamic, powerful, effective prayer focuses on the specific need of the one for whom intercession is offered. It is formed by our attempt to discern what it would mean for the kingdom to break into the present situation. In so doing, it voices the cry for the kingdom in a specific manner.

Let us be encouraged in interceding for others, knowing that such prayer brings results. The mother of Augustine interceded with God for fifteen years on behalf of her son. Eventually her prayers carried the day. Augustine came to know the Lord. He then went on to become one of the greatest theologians the church has produced.

2. Praying for the World Situation: Evangelization

Just as we can pray boldly on behalf of specific individuals who have not yet given their lives to Christ, so also we can bring before our God the need of the world. In the midst of the evil present in society, we can be about the task of petitioning our heavenly Father with Jesus' words, "Your will be done on earth as it is in heaven." We can pray for the in-breaking of the kingdom into our world. One crucial aspect of prayer for the world situation focuses on the evangelization of the entire world.

To this end, we are entrusted with the privilege of interceding for political leaders. Paul enjoins this task in his instruction to Timothy: "I urge, then, first of all, that requests, prayers, intercession and thanksgiving be made for everyone — for kings, and all those in authority" (1 Tim. 2:1-2a). Paul clarifies, however, that intercession for those in authority has a specific purpose in view: ". . . that we may live peaceful and quiet lives in all godliness and holiness" (v. 2). We pray for political leaders in part because of the role that they play in maintaining peace and security. We invoke the Spirit of wisdom in their lives so that they may be able to advance the cause of peace.

The coming of peace *(shalom)* is in keeping with God's intention for human relationships. Nevertheless, Paul has another end in view: "This is good, and pleases God our Savior, who wants all people to be saved and to come to a knowledge of the truth" (1 Tim. 2:3-4, NIV ILE). Paul indicates that our intent in praying for peace is not so that we might live comfortably. Rather, peace is important to the unbridled proclamation of the gospel. During times of war the gospel is proclaimed, of course, and people respond. But in general, war hinders the work of evangelism. It is during times of peace and stability that Christians are most free to proclaim the good news to others. Because proclamation most readily occurs when the world is enjoying peace, we advance the cause of the evangelization of the world by interceding for political leaders.

Several years ago, the World Literature Crusade (now known as Every Home for Christ) set as its goal the blanketing of the earth with the gospel of Christ. To this end, this organization has suggested seven petitions that we should offer on behalf of world leaders.[8] First, "pray that leaders who govern unjustly will make many mistakes in decisions that involve world evangelism" (Ps. 109:3-4, 29). Second, "pray that leaders who despise God and his Son will fall from power through improper advice" (Ps. 5:10; 2 Sam. 15:31). Third, "pray that leaders who are truly searching for understanding will find knowledge and wisdom in God's word" (Prov. 28:2). Fourth, "pray that leaders who live in darkness will receive a personal message of God's love" (Isa. 52:15). Fifth, "pray that leaders who live in war-torn nations will grow weary of the continual bloodshed" (1 Kings 5:3-4). Sixth, "pray that leaders who head corrupt governments will recognize their evil ways and turn to God" (2 Chron. 33:12-13). Finally, "pray that leaders who boast of their power will realize their earthly kingdom was given to them by God" (Dan. 2:9-22; Prov. 21:1). The same God who urged the Old Testament people of God to "pray for the peace of Jerusalem" (Ps. 122:6) calls upon Christ's church to pray for the peace of the world.

Yet our prayer for the evangelization of the world ought to move beyond prayer for world leaders. Our responsibility includes petitioning God regarding the various aspects involved in completing the task of the proclamation of the gospel. We know that prayer directed to this end is in keeping with the will of God because Jesus declared that the

8. What follows is summarized from Dick Eastman, "The Sevenfold World Leaders Prayer Focus," in the World Literature Crusade pamphlet titled "Kings and Presidents."

good news of the kingdom would be preached in the whole world before the end of the age would come (Matt. 24:14). Our Lord's words suggest that his glorious return will not occur until the gospel blankets the earth.

To this end, Jesus gave to his disciples the mandate of the Great Commission: "Therefore go and make disciples of all nations, baptizing them in the name of the Father and of the Son and of the Holy Spirit, and teaching them to obey everything I have commanded you. And surely I will be with you always, to the very end of the age" (Matt. 28:19-20). Jesus' commission ends with the glorious promise that he will be present with his disciples in this task. In fact, through his Spirit, the risen Lord is the one who is ultimately at work in the expansion of the gospel. "I will build my church," Jesus promised, and his presence with us means that even the gates of Hades will not withstand the church's onslaught (Matt. 16:18).

Not only should Christians pray for the evangelization of the world in general; they should also intercede for Christ's emissaries. One early missionary, the apostle Paul, offered what might be seen as a model prayer for interceding for missionaries: "Finally, brothers and sisters, pray for us that the message of the Lord may spread rapidly and be honored, just as it was with you. And pray that we may be delivered from wicked and evil people, for not everyone has faith" (2 Thess. 3:1-2, NIV ILE). Note that this prayer contains two central requests. We are to pray that the missionaries' words will be energized, so that the message will spread. And we are to petition our heavenly Father that Christ's emissaries be protected from their enemies.[9] These two petitions ought to be offered continually for every missionary sent out by the body of Christ.

In addition to praying for those who have already been sent, we ought not to forget to pray for ongoing missionary recruitment. Jesus gave this command to his disciples: "The harvest is plentiful but the workers are few. Ask the Lord of the harvest, therefore, to send out workers into his harvest field" (Matt. 9:37-38). As in Jesus' day, our world is ready to hear the good news. What is desperately needed is a

9. Dick Eastman offers an alternate list of proper requests: for workers for the harvest, for open doors, for abiding fruit, and for a strong support base. See Eastman, *The Hour That Changes the World* (Grand Rapids: Baker, 1978), pp. 153-57.

cadre of persons who are willing to cross cultural boundaries to proclaim the gospel. Whether or not you and I are specifically called to vocational missionary service, we share the joyous task of petitioning the Lord to raise up those who are.

3. Praying for the World Situation: Social Action

The gospel is not only directed to the reconciliation of individual human beings with God. Its goal includes reconciliation within the human family and between humankind and creation. For this reason, the task of the people of God in partnership with the Holy Spirit entails the advancement of God's rule in the realms of social justice and ecology. These are also central to the kingdom of God. Kenneth Leech points out the basically spiritual nature of such activity: "So in the spiritual life we are not only concerned with personal freedom, but also with freedom in social structures, and with deliverance from social paralysis."[10]

Prayer is a powerful weapon in this endeavor. In describing prayer as political action, Eugene H. Peterson claims that "far more of our nation's life is shaped by prayer than is formed by legislation."[11] Whether or not Peterson is speaking hyperbolically, he is surely correct that prayer must play an important role in Christian involvement in attempts to foster the transformation of society. Donald Bloesch remarks,

> Although it is the highest form of action, prayer is not the only form of Christian action. Deeds of lovingkindness and works of social reform also comprise a necessary part of Christian life, but they must always be informed by prayer. It can be said that the glory of God is the goal of prayer; social service is the fruit or consequence of prayer.[12]

10. Leech, *True Prayer* (New York: Harper & Row, 1980), p. 69.

11. Peterson, *Earth and Altar: The Community of Prayer in a Self-Bound Society* (Downers Grove, Ill.: InterVarsity Press, 1985), p. 15.

12. Bloesch, *The Struggle of Prayer* (San Francisco: Harper & Row, 1980), pp. 131-32.

With this statement Bloesch highlights one important facet of the role of prayer in this task. Social concern arises out of an awareness of the "not yet" status of the world in every current form. The arrival of God's kingdom in its fullness awaits Jesus' return. But the vision of that glorious future day can form both the motivation and the blueprint for Christian social involvement in the present.

Prayer is one means that God's Spirit uses in illuminating our hearts and minds to understand the church's task in the present situation. Through prayer, the Spirit leads us to see anew the glorious biblical vision of God's rule and to perceive the depth to which our social situation falls short of that vision. Here again, Leech's words are helpful:

> He is the Spirit of the Age to Come, the initiator of a new order where young men shall see visions and old men shall dream dreams. Prayer which lacks this future orientation is bound to become settled and at ease, a victim of that false peace against which the prophets constantly warn us.[13]

The Spirit's goal is not merely to bring us to see the discrepancy between our present reality and God's future ideal. Rather, through prayer, the Spirit renews in us a longing for the coming kingdom of God, a longing that leads us to desire the in-breaking of the future into the present. And by means of prayer, the Spirit brings us to the place where we are willing to commit ourselves to positive engagement in our world as agents of God's transformation of society in accordance with the ideal of the future kingdom. In prayer, we are strengthened for service, renewed in faith, and empowered to engage in kingdom work within our fallen and sinful world.

There is, however, yet another dimension, one that we easily overlook. In the context of social engagement, prayer is also actual spiritual battle. When we seek to minister to the needs of others and to bring about social transformation, we soon discover that we are confronted by immovable structures that lie beyond our ability to overcome. In the struggle against such seemingly obdurate powers, we come to appreciate the profundity of Paul's appraisal of the context in which we minis-

---

13. Leech, *True Prayer*, p. 68.

ter: "For our struggle is not against flesh and blood, but against the rulers, against the authorities, against the powers of this dark world and against the spiritual forces of evil in the heavenly realms" (Eph. 6:12).

When we come up against these powerful forces, we must depend solely on divine power and seek even the direct intervention of God. In such situations, petition takes on a new and deeper meaning as we come to realize that the resources that can carry the day are released only through prayer. For this reason, Paul admonishes us, "pray in the Spirit on all occasions with all kinds of prayers and requests" (Eph. 6:18). In petitionary prayer we tap the power of God, the power of the kingdom, which alone is able "to demolish strongholds" (2 Cor. 10:4).

Here, as in other situations, our prayer moves in two directions. Prayer becomes a means, coupled with Bible study, for discerning the will of God. Through prayer, we come to appraise the current world order in the light of the biblical vision of the future new order. As we petition the coming of God's rule, as we pray "your kingdom come, your will be done on earth as it is in heaven," the Spirit illumines our minds to see what it would mean if the structures of our world were to be transformed in accordance with the will of God. Prayer likewise becomes the plea for God to act in the present situation: it becomes the cry for the kingdom, based on our realization that only God's power is sufficient to overcome the "spiritual forces of evil." As our praying moves in these two directions, it lays hold of and releases God's willingness and power to act in accordance with God's own glorious will — in accordance with the kingdom of God — on behalf of the creation that God loves.

4. Praying for Other Christians

In addition to being concerned for persons who have not committed their lives to Christ and for the world situation as a whole, the Bible admonishes us to intercede on behalf of one another. Hubert Northcott goes so far as to declare that intercession ought to be "first and foremost for the members of the Church."[14]

14. Northcott, *Man, God, and Prayer* (London: SPCK, 1962), pp. 148-51. See also

Interceding for fellow believers is a crucial aspect of our calling to be the "priesthood of believers."[15] This biblical concept declares that in an important way each Christian is to function as a "priest." To understand what this involves requires that we remind ourselves of what priests in ancient Israel did. According to the Old Testament, priests offered sacrifices to God and interceded on behalf of others. According to the New Testament, Christians are to engage in similar acts. We are to offer spiritual sacrifices to God, including praise and thanksgiving, through such practices as singing, testifying, and individual and communal prayer. The New Testament likewise entrusts to Christians the second priestly function: intercession on behalf of others. To us has been given the great privilege of bringing each other's needs to God in prayer.

As with all petitionary prayer, our intercession for each other should be informed by our desire to pray according to God's will and hence to invoke the in-breaking of the kingdom into the present situation. Consequently, praying effectively necessitates that we continually ask, What is God's will in this situation?

There are two major aspects of God's will for Christians. The first is what is often referred to as "God's general will." This includes the development in us of the various spiritual traits that ought to characterize our lives. Paul declares that God's will for us all is that we grow toward spiritual maturity — that is, that we become mature in faith, knowledge, doctrine, character, and speech (Eph. 4:13-15). Consequently, we may boldly direct our intercession for each other toward this goal, knowing that such prayer is in accordance with the will of God. Our intercession could follow this pattern: "Father, may your Spirit be at work in the life of my Christian friend, causing her to grow to maturity. May she be built up in the faith and in her knowledge of you. May she hold fast to correct doctrine. May her character increasingly conform to that of Jesus, and may her speech always be the truth seasoned with love."

In addition to God's general will, we routinely speak about God's specific or individual will. Whereas God's desire that we grow in grace

---

Kornelis H. Miskotte, *The Roads of Prayer,* trans. John W. Doberstein (New York: Sheed & Ward, 1968), pp. 65-67.

15. For a discussion of this concept and its basis in the Old Testament role of intercessors, see Lukas Vischer, *Intercession* (Geneva: World Council of Churches, 1980), pp. 25-27, 48-49.

is universal, our loving heavenly Father also has intentions that are unique to each believer. These include such matters as vocational calling and place of service. We can intercede for each other in this aspect of God's will as well. We ask God to lead our brothers and sisters in Christ to find specific places of service. We pray as well that the Holy Spirit strengthen them in the face of the struggles of life, so that we might all remain faithful in our divinely given roles and in the specific tasks to which the Spirit has called each of us.

Jesus' example of special concern for his disciples is instructive for us as we seek to intercede for each other. In his "high priestly prayer," our Lord declared to his heavenly Father, "My prayer is not that you take them out of the world but that you protect them from the evil one. They are not of the world, even as I am not of it. Sanctify them by the truth; your word is truth" (John 17:15-17). Following Jesus' example would lead us to avoid asking God simply to grant each of us a life of ease. We would not petition God to spare us from the trials of life. Rather, our intercession would focus on invoking God's protecting presence in the face of Satan's onslaught. We would also invite the Spirit's sanctifying work in us, so that we might all be built up through the truth that is God's Word.

We can gain additional insight into the task of intercession by noting the prayers that are found in the New Testament writings. Paul begins nearly all of his letters by interceding for his readers.[16] Other New Testament texts reflect the petitions that lay on the authors' hearts.[17] We do well to let the prayers of Paul and other biblical writers teach us how to intercede for one another. Such prayers indicate what petitions are in keeping with God's will for his children. They show us how to invoke the in-breaking of the kingdom in each other's lives.

5. Praying in Situations in Which God's Will Is Not Known

Effective prayer is prayer that is in accordance with God's will, prayer that invokes the in-breaking of the kingdom into the present. In many

---

16. E.g., Eph. 1:15-19; Phil. 1:9-11; Col. 1:9-12; 2 Thess. 1:12; Philemon 6.
17. See Eph. 6:18; Rom. 15:5-6, 13; 2 Cor. 13:7; Eph. 3:16-19; 1 Thess. 3:10-13; 5:23; 2 Thess. 2:17; 3:5, 16; Heb. 13:21.

situations of life, we can readily discern the will of God. But what about the many occasions in which we simply do not know what God's complete will is? Let me suggest that even then, we can pray in accordance with God's will. Above all, three needs, which are present in nearly every situation, can become the focus of fruitful petition.

First, we can always petition God regarding those aspects of the divine will that we do know are appropriate to the situation. Often we find ourselves in circumstances in which we feel that we are in the dark regarding the divine plan. Yet if we look more closely, we discover that we are not wandering around in total darkness. On the contrary, we see that we are, in fact, cognizant of some aspects of God's will. These can become topics of bold, believing prayer.

For example, in the midst of sickness or tribulation, we can always pray that the adverse circumstance will bring about spiritual growth. We can pray in this manner because we know that God intends such growth as a by-product of enduring trial (James 1:2-4). This spiritual truth, therefore, can form the basis for petitioning God to produce growth in us or in others. In addition, we can pray that the joy of the Lord be present in the midst of adversity, for this too is God's will (1 Pet. 1:6-7; Rom. 5:3-5).

Second, in every situation we can pray for wisdom and discernment. When we find ourselves unable to discern the divine will, we can petition the Giver of wisdom for insight. James writes, "If any of you lacks wisdom, you should ask God, who gives generously to all without finding fault, and it will be given to you" (James 1:5, NIV ILE). On the basis of this biblical admonition we know that God desires to answer the prayer for wisdom.

Situations in which we do not know God's will require patient resting in the Lord and confident trusting that God's answer will come. In such circumstances, we become especially vulnerable to the temptation to grow weary of waiting for divine direction. In our impatience we attempt to run ahead of God, or we find ourselves becoming anxious. In addition to the prayer for wisdom, therefore, we can boldly request that we be granted the patience that the Spirit provides, so that we will be able to "wait on the Lord," knowing the truth of Isaiah's words: "Those who hope in the LORD will renew their strength" (Isa. 40:31a; cf. Phil. 4:6-7).

Third, when God's complete will has not yet been revealed to us, we can nevertheless pray that the Spirit would plant within our hearts a willingness to accept the divine will when it is finally revealed. In fact, it might be that God is waiting for such an expression of our personal willingness before revealing to us the hidden aspects of the divine plan. Sometimes God withholds knowledge of his will from us simply because he knows that we are not yet ready to embrace the next stage of his perfect plan for us. In such a situation, prayer becomes not only the struggle to discern God's will but also the struggle to become willing to obey it when God chooses to reveal it to us. Sometimes, it is only when we release ourselves into the hand of God and pledge ourselves to obeying his undisclosed will that the light finally dawns in our souls.

Praying for the Sick

One of the most difficult circumstances that we face is physical sickness. The fact that people get sick challenges not only our understanding of how prayer works but also our willingness to pray. The Gospels and the book of Acts are filled with stories of healings. And James provides a specific model as to how to pray for the sick. Nevertheless, the practice of what is often called "healing prayer" is largely overlooked in most congregations.[18] Some Christians find the stories of healings that appear repeatedly in Scripture puzzling or even embarrassing. And many members of more traditional churches dismiss any suggestion that prayer can play a direct role in physical healing as "charismatic enthusiasm." Despite this long-standing skepticism or even aversion to the idea, the concept of healing prayer has gained renewed interest in recent decades, not only in the church but also in the wider society and even among medical practitioners.

1. The Causes of Sickness

According to the Bible, the ultimate cause of sickness is human sin. The presence of disease in our world is an evil effect of the primordial

---

18. Gordon Dalbey, "Recovering Healing Prayer," *Christian Century*, 9 June 1982, pp. 690-93.

fall. We know that susceptibility to illness is not God's ultimate will for us, because one glorious day when the kingdom of God comes in its fullness, God will banish sickness from the new creation. Until then, the presence of disease is a constant reminder of the fallenness of this world.

All sickness is the result of the fall. Yet, when we get sick, a more specific cause is generally at work. Sometimes we become ill for no other reason than because we live in a fallen environment. Sin has affected the entire cosmos (Rom. 8:18-22), and as a consequence, we get sick. At other times, the sicknesses that come our way may be due to the fact that we live in the society that we do. Certain illnesses are endemic to particular societies. In a sense, they arise as an outworking of the values, actions, character, and even the sins of that society. For example, the 1960s brought a marked increase in leukemia cases in the United States that was due in part to the atomic bomb testing that had been conducted in the western states during the Cold War era. More recently, factors such as the pace of life, the diet, and the success of the fast-food industry have resulted in a surge of a variety of diseases, some of which are linked to obesity, that are largely unknown in other parts of the world.

Not to be overlooked is a third cause: personal sin. Some of the sicknesses that we contract are caused by the sins of others. Exposure to secondhand smoke, to cite an obvious example, can lead to lung cancer. Aspects of our own chosen lifestyle, especially insofar as we persist in potentially harmful practices, can likewise make us susceptible to certain illnesses. Thus, alcohol abuse can lead to liver problems, overeating to high blood pressure, and sexual licentiousness to sexually transmitted diseases, including HIV/AIDS.

There is yet a fourth cause, however — one that we do not always consider. A sickness might come our way as an aspect of God's response to some specific sin that we have committed. Paul reports that some members of the Corinthian church had become sick because they had desecrated the Lord's Supper. In fact, in several cases, their actions had even resulted in death (1 Cor. 11:30).[19]

19. Various understandings present in the New Testament are evaluated by Robert M. Price in "Illness Theodicies in the New Testament," *Journal of Religion and Health* 25, no. 4 (1986): 309-15.

Of course, not every sickness is the direct result of personal sin. We dare not conclude that each sick person we meet has committed some vile act. Jesus' statement to his disciples when they came upon a man who had been blind since birth should quickly dispel this idea. In response to their query, "Rabbi, who sinned, this man or his parents, that he was born blind?" Jesus answered, "Neither this man nor his parents sinned . . . but this happened so that the work of God might be displayed in his life" (John 9:2-3).

2. Sickness and God's Will

Jesus' declaration that the man's blindness was designed to be the occasion for a demonstration of God's work in his life leads us to the controversial question of the relationship between sickness and God's will.

Some Christians claim that sickness is never part of the divine plan, so that in every situation healing should come. They believe that God's will for us is that we be physically whole, not only in the glorious future kingdom of God but already in this life. The Chinese devotional writer Watchman Nee drew this perspective from Isaiah's declaration regarding the coming of the Suffering Servant: "By his wounds we are healed" (Isa. 53:4-5). Nee declared that Christ bore not only our sins but also our sicknesses on the cross. As a consequence of Christ's atoning work, Nee concluded, "Both the healing of the body and the peace of the soul are accorded us."[20]

Many faith healers base their ministry on a similar understanding of God's will for us and of the extent of Christ's work. Some then go so far as to assert that the prayer that is offered in genuine faith will always result in healing. This implies, of course, that people who do not experience healing lack sufficient faith. What this widely propagated belief overlooks is the fact that although unbelief can be a detriment to God's miraculous intervention in our lives, many other factors might preclude a prayer for healing from evoking an affirmative response.

The Bible declares that sickness will be banished from God's eternal

20. Watchman Nee, *The Spiritual Man* (New York: Christian Fellowship Publishers, 1968), 3:159. Nee offers an interesting and helpful discussion of sickness in this volume (3:158-95).

kingdom (Rev. 21:4). In the meantime, however, illness is a reality of human existence. Although sickness is an evil, like other trials, it can be overruled for good. God is so great that he can use illness to accomplish his good purposes. Illness can occasion spiritual growth in us, and it can lead to the strengthening of our faith.

At times, God may also use sickness as a way of disciplining us. God's intent may be to warn us of the presence of sin in our lives or to foster repentance in us. Just as the nervous system in the body utilizes pain to warn of a deeper problem, so also sickness can be a warning of an inner spiritual problem, as in the case of the Corinthian church (see also James 5:14-16).

Whatever the cause, all sickness can bring positive benefits. Illness is always evil. Yet God is able to bring good out of evil. As Paul declared to the Romans, "And we know that in all things God works for the good of those who love him, who have been called according to his purpose" (Rom. 8:28). Believers throughout the ages have testified to this truth. Many have gained positive personal benefit through suffering. Others have been strengthened in faith by observing the steadfast endurance of those who have gone through the valley of the shadow of death or of those who have given personal evidence to the strengthening power and compassionate care that God provides.

3. Prayer for the Sick

With these considerations regarding the causes and purposes of illness in view, we are in a position to consider how we might best pray for the sick. It is not surprising that the same basic principle that we have noted regarding prayer in the other circumstances should provide guidance here as well. We know that God will act in response to prayer that is in accordance with the divine will. The key to praying for a sick friend, then, is to discern what God's will is in this particular situation. This suggests two quite different circumstances in which we might be moved to pray for the sick.

Occasionally we will find ourselves interceding for a sick person in a situation in which the illness came as a direct result of his or her sin and in which we have gained assurance from God that the sick friend's confession and repentance will result in divine healing. This is the situation that James has in view when he writes, "Is any one of you sick? Call the elders of the church to pray over you and anoint you with oil in the name of the Lord" (James 5:14, NIV ILE). In this situation, the goal of the illness is to bring about the restoration of the sick person's relationship to God. Once this purpose has been accomplished, the prayer for healing will be effective, for through this prayer, the petitioner lays hold of God's willingness to forgive and heal.

In this process, the prompting of the Holy Spirit in the life of the sick person is crucial. He or she must first come to the awareness that the root problem is some personal sin that needs to be confessed. This must be followed by a willingness to confess and forsake the underlying sin. When this occurs, the leaders of the church can be rallied to intercede on his or her behalf. And their prayer will release God's willingness to restore the wayward believer to health.

When I was the pastor of a local church some years ago, I received a desperate telephone call from a woman in the congregation. Mary had been hospitalized for a routine surgery. But something had gone wrong in the process, and as a result she needed a second surgery. Mary acknowledged to me that she faced the pending procedure with great fear, because she knew in her heart that the mishap was God's attempt to get her attention. In response to her request, I gathered the elders, together with her husband, around Mary's bed. In our presence, she confessed her sin and asked both her husband and God to forgive her. We then anointed her with oil and prayed in great faith that God would heal her. Our prayer was answered. Mary went through surgery with no complications and soon was restored to full health. She left the hospital a changed woman!

Experiences such as this do occur. Yet generally when we are burdened to pray for a sick person, the illness is not part of God's disciplining work in his or her life. Of course, through our intercession we might gain assurance from God that the good that our loving heavenly Father intended to bring out of this evil has been attained and therefore that he will respond to the prayer for healing. When this occurs, we can pray in full confidence that healing will follow.

More often, however, we find ourselves unable to claim any assurance whatsoever that our intercession will result in healing. We simply may not have discerned the mind of God regarding this situation. At such times, we can, of course, take comfort in remembering that even

Paul found it necessary to leave his associate, Trophimus, sick in Miletus (2 Tim. 4:20). These circumstances ought to occasion fervent prayer with the goal of discovering not only God's will but also God's perfect timing in revealing the divine will. In this process, we might repeatedly hear God say, "Not yet." Yet whatever the final outcome of the illness — even if in the end the person dies — we can rest assured that one day God will change the "not yet" of the present to his final "Now!" when we all share in the fullness of the resurrection at our Lord's return.

Even when we cannot offer a prayer for healing with full assurance of God's response, we can voice other requests, knowing that they are in accordance with his will. We can petition God for wisdom. We can ask God to bring some positive good out of the infirmity. As with other trials, sickness may lead to conversion, the strengthening of faith, or spiritual growth. These effects need not be limited to the sick person, but can occur in others as well, including family and friends, medical personnel, other patients, and so forth. We can boldly pray toward this end.

Above all, we can request that God grant spiritual illumination to all persons involved in the situation. We desire that the Spirit illume everyone to see God's strengthening presence so that they can withstand the onslaught of Satan, who seeks to use trial as an occasion to foster discouragement. In this context, Paul's prayer on behalf of the Ephesians is especially appropriate:

> I keep asking that the God of our Lord Jesus Christ, the glorious Father, may give you the Spirit of wisdom and revelation, so that you may know him better. I pray also that the eyes of your heart may be enlightened in order that you may know the hope to which he has called you, the riches of his glorious inheritance in the saints, and his incomparably great power for us who believe. That power is like the working of his mighty strength, which he exerted in Christ when he raised him from the dead and seated him at his right hand in the heavenly realms, far above all rule and authority, power and dominion, and every title that can be given, not only in the present age but also in the one to come. (Eph. 1:17-21)

When we as concerned intercessors follow Paul's example, our prayer releases God's willingness and power to encourage those who are despairing in the face of the trials of life.

All petition is a cry for the kingdom. Yet there is a sense in which this is true of prayer for the sick in a special way. The fallenness of creation due to sin is vividly seen and experienced through physical ailments and death. Petition in the face of sickness, therefore, provides an appropriate occasion to echo the second petition of the Lord's Prayer: "Your kingdom come, your will be done on earth as it is in heaven." Our cry for the in-breaking of the kingdom into this particular experience of the fallenness of the present age elicits God's response. The immediate response may come in the form of restoration of health. Or it may be limited to spiritual strengthening. In either case, we know that the greater divine response is yet future. One day, all of our prayers for healing will be fully answered as death is swallowed up in victory, and all creation is renewed in the glorious kingdom of God.

Praying Specifically

Repeatedly in the foregoing discussions of prayer according to God's will I have alluded to the importance of praying specifically. Rosalind Rinker has been especially forthright in calling Christians to pray in this manner. As she points out in her helpful book, *Prayer: Conversing with God*,[21] many of our prayers are simply too general to be answerable. Rather than taking prayer seriously, we often merely go through the motions of prayer. You can get a sense of whether or not this is true in your praying by asking yourself several questions after you pray. Did I ask God for anything definite? Was I anticipating any definite response from God? How will I be able to determine if God has in fact answered my prayer? And how will I know when the answer has come?

Most of us, if we are honest with ourselves, would have to admit that we often do not take prayer seriously. Nor do we pray expecting anything to occur as a result of our prayer. But why is this the case? And why do Christians pray such general, generic prayers? At times our prayers are general because we voice them without prior thinking. We become caught up in the ritual of prayer, rather than engaging in an exercise of faith in which we truly believe that God will respond to our petitions.

21. Rinker, *Prayer: Conversing with God* (Grand Rapids: Zondervan, 1959).

Actually, we often find ourselves in a vicious cycle. We do not pray specifically because we do not believe that God will answer; but we do not believe that God will answer because we ask for nothing specific. To see if this is true in your life, ask yourself the next time you pray, Do I genuinely believe that God will do this? James tells us that when we ask, we must believe and not doubt, for otherwise we are "like a wave of the sea, blown and tossed by wind" (James 1:6).

To counteract our seemingly innate tendency toward general, generic praying, Rinker suggests a technique that involves making "faith-sized requests."[22] A faith-sized request is one that is the right size for your faith. It is not so large that its very size causes you to wonder if God will answer. Rather, in each situation you ask only for what you really believe God will in fact do. The request ought to be small enough that it can be offered in genuine faith: "Father, to be completely honest, I do not think you would respond to a big request. But I am convinced you would be willing to do this small thing." Of course, one goal for prayer is that our faith might be deepened as we come to a fuller understanding of the nature of God's will. Yet, en route to this goal we might find it helpful to begin by petitioning God with requests that are small enough that we can offer them in faith.

Rinker also encourages petitioners to "climb the steps of prayer."[23] A chain of faith-sized requests makes a large request more manageable and detailed. She cites by way of example a young couple that moved into a new neighborhood with the goal of winning their neighbors to the Lord. Rather than offering the general prayer "Lord, save our neighbors," they tackled the situation step by step. The first step came with the husband praying, "Lord, I would like to meet the fellow living next door in some casual way and begin to get acquainted with him." That request was met as their children quarreled over a tricycle. The second step followed: "Lord, I would like to know what that man is interested in so we could become friends." Soon the answer came — football. Now the Christian man boldly took the third step: "Lord, I need two complimentary football tickets, and could I have them by this weekend, please?" God provided the tickets, and the friendship grew. In this way, these Christians prayed step by step

22. Rinker, *Prayer,* p. 73.
23. Rinker, *Prayer,* p. 76.

for their neighbors, who eventually became part of the family of God.[24]

Faith is a significant prerequisite for successful prayer. But the key to praying in faith rests in coming to know more and more about God's will and God's nature. The biblical promise is clear: "This is the assurance we have in approaching God: that if we ask anything according to his will, he hears us. And if we know that he hears us — whatever we ask — we know that we have what we asked of him" (1 John 5:14-15). We can ask in faith when we come to understand the will of God, for prayer is laying hold of God's willingness to act in accordance with the divine will. When we do so, we can enjoy great confidence in prayer. And such confidence leads us boldly to the cry for the kingdom, to invoke the in-breaking of God's reign into whatever situation — large or small — we find ourselves facing.

24. Rinker, *Prayer,* pp. 76-77.

5. Persisting in Prayer

In these pages, I have repeatedly declared that ultimately prayer is the cry for the kingdom. It is the request that the future reign of God break into the situations that we face in the present. Moreover, I have indicated that supplication lays hold of and releases God's willingness to act in accordance with the divine will. This chapter develops further this understanding of prayer by engaging a crucial question regarding the practice of the kind of prayer that I have been presenting: Should we bring a particular request to God more than once? That is, should we be persistent in our praying? At first glance, this query appears quite simple. At a deeper level, however, it touches our entire outlook regarding the nature of prayer.

Some Christians would respond to my question with an immediate "No!" In their estimation, to bring a specific request to God more than once is to give evidence to a lack of faith in God. "Badgering" God with the same petition, they argue, indicates that we do not really believe that God's answer is forthcoming. Similarly, failing simply to leave the matter with God, once we have voiced our need in his presence, reveals that deep inside we doubt God's love and goodness. If we truly believe that God has heard our prayer, they advise, we can trust God to answer in his good time and in his good way. Therefore, anything more than a one-time supplication borders on sin. In support of this perspective, these Christians cite a statement from our Lord, which they interpret as a warning against repetitive praying: "Do not keep on babbling like pagans, for they think they will be heard because of their many words" (Matt. 6:7).

Considerations such as these might have some merit, at least in certain situations. Nevertheless, I am convinced that persistency in prayer can be thoroughly biblical and experientially beneficial. In fact, the very nature and purpose of supplication mandates that we persist in prayer before God. Prayer is not simply the cry for the kingdom; it is a *continual* cry. As we repeatedly pray "Your kingdom come, your will be done" in the various circumstances that we face, we are enabled by the Spirit to know and affirm God's will for our lives, for the church, and for the entire world.

Jesus' Command to Persistency

On at least two occasions, Jesus instructed his followers to be persistent in prayer. The first is found in a section of Luke's Gospel devoted to Jesus' teaching on prayer that followed the giving of the Lord's Prayer: "So I say to you: Ask and it will be given to you; seek and you will find; knock and the door will be opened to you. For everyone who asks receives; everyone who seeks finds; and to everyone who knocks, the door will be opened" (Luke 11:9-10, NIV ILE; parallel text, Matt. 7:7-11).

This statement, which we might describe as Jesus' "command to persistency," is preceded by a parable and followed by a series of analogies. The parable Jesus tells sets the context for the admonition. It focuses on a householder who was surprised by a late-night visitor and, to remedy this plight, sought help from a neighbor at an inopportune time:

> Then he said to them, "Suppose one of you has a friend, and he goes to him at midnight and says, 'Friend, lend me three loaves of bread, because a friend of mine on a journey has come to me, and I have nothing to set before him.'
>
> "Then the one inside answers, 'Don't bother me. The door is already locked, and my children are with me in bed. I can't get up and give you anything.'" I tell you, though he will not get up and give him the bread because he is his friend, yet because of the man's persistence he will get up and give him as much as he needs." (Luke 11:5-8)

In his widely read *Daily Study Bible,* William Barclay provides some of the pertinent details that lie behind this parable.[1] The story opens

---

1. Barclay, *The Daily Study Bible: The Gospel of Luke* (Toronto: G. R. Welch Co., Ltd., 1975), pp. 145-46.

with the late arrival of a traveler at the house of a friend. This situation was not unusual. In the first century, travelers often journeyed late into the evening in order to avoid the heat of the daytime sun. In the ancient world, providing hospitality to weary travelers was considered obligatory. And hospitality meant that a host could not offer merely minimal provisions, but would have an obligation to make available to the traveler an abundance of food and a comfortable place to stay.

To prevent bread from becoming stale and inedible, people in those days tended to bake every day. And they baked only what they thought they would need for the day. In Jesus' story, the late arrival of the traveler put the householder in an embarrassing situation. He was unable to provide the abundance that hospitality required. His sense of obligation drove him to seek the assistance of a friend.

The typical house in first-century Palestine consisted of one large room. During the day, the door to the house would remain open. A shut door, therefore, was a sign that the householder did not want to be disturbed. In the story, the friend's door had been shut, indicating that the family had gone to bed for the night.

The typical single-room house was divided into two sections. One part of the room, which was generally raised slightly, contained the stove, around which the entire family slept on mats. Consequently, if one family member should awaken and rise, they would all inevitably be disturbed.

The householder who went to seek aid from his friend knocked at his door relentlessly and voiced his request repeatedly. It is likely that such obnoxious boldness would disturb not only the father but the entire family, as well as whatever animals were also in the house. We can therefore imagine that the whole household was now not only awake but also verbalizing their annoyance. With his family up in arms, the friend relented and gave his neighbor whatever leftover provisions remained in the house. The householder's persistence had eventually done the trick.

The other bookend for Jesus' "command to persistence" is a series of analogies that provided the theological basis for both the point made in the parable and our Lord's admonitions: "Which of you fathers, if your son asks for a fish, will give him a snake instead? Or if he asks for an egg, will give him a scorpion? If you then, though you are evil, know how to give good gifts to your children, how much more will

your Father in heaven give the Holy Spirit to those who ask him!"
(Luke 11:11-13).

Barclay's commentary on the parallel text in Matthew 7 — which
adds the query "Which of you, if his son asks for bread, will give him a
stone?" (v. 9) — explains the significance of the analogies that Jesus
chose.[2] The stone may have been one of the limestone pebbles found on
the Palestine seashore that were the shape and color of little loaves of
bread. The snake was perhaps an eel, which according to Jewish food
laws was an unclean fish and therefore inedible (Lev. 11:12). The scorpion was especially dangerous, because of the deadly sting lodged in its
tail, which it would bring over its back to strike its victim. When a scorpion was resting, its claws and tail were folded in so that it looked
something like an egg.

Jesus' point in each analogy is the same. Human fathers do not
mock their children by giving them something that resembles what
they ask for but is in fact dangerous. Even more so, the Father of Jesus'
disciples will not mock them when they pray. God will never respond to
them by offering something that appears similar to the requested provision but is unbeneficial or even harmful.

Jesus' characterization of God as the one who does not mock the
prayers of his children forms a sharp contrast to the manner in which
the Greek gods were believed to act. The stories of the deities that the
Greeks told often portray the gods as responding to petitions in a way
that ultimately proved harmful. In one story, the goddess of the dawn,
Aurora, fell in love with a human youth, Tithonus. Zeus offered to give
Tithonus any one gift that Aurora would choose for her lover. Aurora
requested that Tithonus live forever. Unfortunately, however, Aurora
failed to specify that what she meant was that Tithonus should remain
forever young. Her request was granted, but in an unfortunate way.
Poor Tithonus grew older and older, but he could not die. Zeus's gift
turned out to be a curse.[3]

Sandwiched between the parable and the analogies is Jesus' admonition: "Ask . . . seek . . . knock" (Luke 11:9). Both evangelists use
present-tense imperatives to give in Greek the sense of Jesus' words. In

2. Barclay, *The Daily Study Bible: The Gospel of Matthew*, 2d ed., 2 vols. (Edinburgh: St. Andrew Press, 1958), 1:274-75.

3. Barclay, *The Daily Study Bible: The Gospel of Matthew*, 1:275.

the Greek language of the day, the present tense generally indicates that the action is being depicted as continuous rather than as occurring at a single point. To give the sense that arises from the Gospel writers' use of the present tense, we might translate Jesus' words this way: "Keep on asking, and it will be given to you. Keep on seeking, and you will find. Keep on knocking, and the door will be opened to you." In short, persistency will bring positive results.

Jesus' command to persistency is predicated on the particular understanding of God that our Lord consistently proclaimed. He pointed to a loving Father who desires and is able to give good things to his children. The realization that God loves us and is willing to give what is good for us ought to lead us to persistency in prayer as well. Yet such knowledge also places an important limitation on prayer. Because our heavenly Father is good, not evil, we can expect him to give us only what is good, only what is in accordance with his holy character. For this reason, we can rightfully be persistent only in requesting good things from God.

The Bible offers numerous illustrations of this principle. Balaam asked God to let him die like a righteous person (Num. 23:10). But because the prophet remained unrepentant, granting this request would have violated God's integrity. Similarly, Jesus could not honor the request of James and John to sit at his right and left in the kingdom (Matt. 20:28), for doing so would have condoned their misunderstanding of prominence.

Jesus instructed his disciples to persist in prayer on another occasion as well — namely, in the parable of the persistent widow:

> "In a certain town there was a judge who neither feared God nor cared about people. And there was a widow in that town who kept coming to him with the plea, 'Grant me justice against my adversary.'
>
> "For some time he refused. But finally he said to himself, 'Even though I don't fear God or care about people, yet because this widow keeps bothering me, I will see that she gets justice, so that she won't eventually wear me out with her coming!'" (Luke 18:2-5, NIV ILE)

To understand this parable, we must read it within the context in which Jesus gave it. Our Lord had just engaged in an extended discourse regarding his future return (Luke 17:20-37) that was triggered by the Pharisees' question as to when the kingdom of God would come. In his initial answer, Jesus spoke about the nature of his return and the conditions that will surround it. At this point, he turned his attention to his disciples and narrated the parable. Then Jesus returned to the topic of his future return, this time, however, posing a terse, crucial question to his audience: "However, when the Son of Man comes, will he find faith on the earth?" (Luke 18:8b). The context of the parable indicates that it too centers on the Lord's glorious return.

The parable features a widow who was the victim of an undisclosed injustice. In an attempt to obtain justice, she repeatedly appealed to a judge to hear her case. Although the judge was not a righteous person, eventually the widow's persistence was rewarded. At the conclusion of the parable, Jesus discloses its point: If sustained pleading can move an unrighteous judge to grant a hapless widow justice, how much more will God, the righteous judge, hear the unfailing pleas of Jesus' oppressed disciples and bring justice to the world? The context of the parable clearly indicates that the response that Jesus was envisioning is the coming of the Son of Man as judge at the end of the age. Hence, God will honor our persistency in praying for the Lord's return. Our cry for the kingdom will not go unheeded.

The primary implication of the parable, therefore, is persistent prayer for the return of Christ. Yet there may be within the story a secondary application as well: persistency as a principle of all praying. Insofar as all our petition is ultimately a cry for the kingdom — a voicing of the plea "Your kingdom come, your will be done on earth as it is in heaven" — we can persist in every such prayer that we bring to our heavenly Father. Not only can we be assured that God's rule will one day come in its fullness; we can anticipate the in-breaking of the power of God into the situations we face in the present.

The key to persistent prayer, however, is to pray according to God's will. We can persist when we know that our prayer is in accordance with the divine purposes. Such prayer will lay hold of and release God's willingness to act.

The Importance of Persistency

Persistency in prayer is biblical. It carries the command of Jesus himself. But why does our Lord admonish his disciples to persist? Why is it often necessary to bring a request to God repeatedly? In what sense is this beneficial? Let me enumerate five benefits that come to us when we pray persistently and then describe an all-encompassing benefit of persistent prayer.

First, when we remain steadfast in prayer, our faith grows. Such growth occurs in part because God's "not yet" — the seemingly endless time when God seems to be silent — often becomes a time in which our faith is tested. When our heavenly Father does not seem to be hearing or answering our petition, we are tempted to question his faithfulness to us his children. It is precisely during such times of temptation and doubt that returning to our knees becomes so important. Continuing to petition God when the answer does not seem to be on the horizon is itself an act of faith. When we persist in prayer, we are in fact exercising our faith. And the Holy Spirit responds by strengthening that faith.

Second, persistency can lead to patience. We live in a "fast-food" society in which patience has become a lost virtue. But God is not a "fast-food" God. The Father of our Lord Jesus gives good gifts to his children in keeping with his good plan for their lives and in accordance with his perfect timing. One of these gifts is patience, a gift that is sometimes bestowed indirectly and unexpectedly. We sometimes receive this gift when we find ourselves waiting for God's response to our petitions for a quite different gift. Moreover, sometimes we sense that God is asking us — even forcing us — to learn to "wait on the Lord." It is, however, in such situations that we come to discover what true waiting entails. Persistency heightens these spiritual experiences that God deems necessary for the development of our character.

Third, persistent praying assists us in the process of determining the extent to which we truly desire and genuinely need what we are requesting. Sometimes our persistency becomes the means whereby we confirm the seriousness of a particular request. Perhaps we can understand why this is so by considering how parents respond to the requests of young children. Good parents do not necessarily rush out to buy a particular toy the first time their child asks for it. Instead, it is the repetition of the request that alerts them that their child's desire for the toy is genuine. The child knows what he or she wants and demonstrates this through the repetition of the request for it. In a somewhat similar manner, our persistency indicates our genuine desire for God to act in a particular way or to meet a particular sensed need.

At other times, persistent prayer becomes the instrument through which we become aware of what we genuinely desire. Again here, the parent-child dynamic can aid our understanding. Children are notorious for requesting that their parents buy them everything that they see. Although this can become wearisome to the parents, it is actually of great benefit to the child. Asking is the process whereby children learn what they truly want and, perhaps more importantly, what they really need. In the process of asking, the child is (even subconsciously) sorting through the various wants and determining which are the most important. In a similar way, we often initially bring a request to God in what is unreflective prayer. But as we continue to bring our particular requests, we are led to sort through the many petitions that we have voiced. As this process continues, some requests fall by the wayside, whereas others come to be articulated with greater fervency. In this manner, we gain insight into what we truly desire. And as this occurs, we are able to measure our desires against God's purposes.

Fourth, perseverance in prayer can foster genuine gratitude for God's provision when it finally comes. In a world of instant gratification, we so often fail to appreciate what easily comes our way. What is received after a time of waiting and intense effort, in contrast, is generally greeted with great thanksgiving. And we often highly treasure such gifts long after they have been given. In a similar manner, through determined petition and patient waiting, we are able to learn true gratitude for what God has done and will do on behalf of his children. Persistent prayer can lead to jubilant joy and hearty thanksgiving when the petition is answered.

Fifth, persistency can be the means through which we come to realize that we have a role to play in the answering of our prayer. As we repeatedly bring the petition to God, we are given occasion to mull over the various aspects of the circumstance about which we are concerned. As we do so, the Holy Spirit is able to illumine our minds and transform our hearts so that we are both able to see and willing to do our part as those who gladly cooperate with God in the in-breaking of the kingdom into the situation of need.

These five beneficial results of persistent prayer are all connected to an important dimension of persistency. They arise out of the fact that persistency requires that we continually voice a request over a period of time. Situations in which God's answer does not come immediately provide the occasion for us to think through our petitions to determine the extent to which our desires reflect kingdom values. This process inaugurates a special kind of conversation with God, a dialogue that could not otherwise occur. Moreover, by means of this conversation we truly become partners with God in the advancement of the kingdom. Persistency in prayer allows us to sift through the present — including our present concerns — and seek to envision what the in-breaking of the kingdom would entail.

This observation leads to the sixth benefit. I have declared repeatedly that prayer releases God's willingness and ability to act. Prayer is especially effective when we know the will of God and can pray confidently that it be done. Whenever we truly know God's will, we can persist in prayer, confident that in God's good timing the answer will come. When we do not know the divine will, persistency in prayer takes on new significance. In such situations, prayer serves as a crucial means for discerning God's will.

Discernment of the divine will comes through persistent prayer in that such prayer provides the space in which the Holy Spirit can bring about changes in the content of our petitions. Through this kind of prayer, the Spirit is able to illumine our minds and redirect the desires of our hearts. The transformation of heart and mind, in turn, leads to praying that is in accordance with the will of God.

When God's answer is not forthcoming, persistent prayer emerges as a conversation with God, or perhaps a dialogue with God's silence. We might describe such prayer in even stronger terms as a struggle to know God's ways and then to affirm God's plan. When this struggle gives way to clarity regarding God's purposes, we come away from the experience with a greater awareness of who God is and a deepened relationship with the God whom we serve. This marks the victory of persistent prayer in our own lives.[4]

4. Donald G. Bloesch, *The Struggle of Prayer* (San Francisco: Harper & Row, 1980), p. 76.

The Persistent Attitude

The pathway of persistent prayer is not always smooth and straight. It has its rough spots as well as its twists and turns. Yet the benefits of persistency are great. Central to both the benefits and the challenges of persistent prayer is what we might call the "persistent attitude."

Perhaps the way to understand what lies at the heart of this attitude is to look again at the arguments against persistency that I mentioned in the opening paragraphs of this chapter. I noted that some Christians claim that repeated asking displays a lack of faith. This argument is erroneous, however, because it would preclude any petitionary prayer whatsoever. Jesus declared that his Father knows the needs of his children before they ask. So if we show a lack of trust by asking God a second and a third time for what we need, we do so if we ask even once. Rather than discouraging us from praying, Jesus saw in the fact that God already knows what we need the very basis for prayer. Indeed, in the Sermon on the Mount, Jesus gave his disciples the Lord's Prayer immediately after declaring, "Your Father knows what you need before you ask him" (Matt. 6:7-9). Rather than showing a lack of faith, persistency reveals a particular kind of faith. The persistent attitude is borne of a faith that steadfastly clings to God's willingness to respond despite present appearances to the contrary. And it occasions an ongoing exercise of faith that the answer will come, even in the face of the present experience of God's silence.

Furthermore, Jesus did not direct his warning regarding "babbling like pagans" (Matt. 6:7) against any repetition in prayer whatsoever. Instead, he was cautioning against the mistaken understanding that suggests that our many words are what insure that God will pay attention to our petitions. Our Lord is reminding us that our praying is not what wins a hearing before God. Hence, we dare not view prayer as "magic," as a way of placing God in our debt, or as a means of manipulating God (which is in fact the essence of the pagan attitude toward the working of prayer). Even when we describe prayer as the laying hold of God's willingness to respond, we must be careful lest we conclude that God's response is due to the sheer fact that we have prayed or because our prayer somehow has intrinsic merit. On the contrary, God responds to prayer out of sovereign grace. God has graciously chosen to use our praying as a means to bring about the divine program.

For this reason, the persistent attitude disavows all self-sufficiency and personal merit. It exchanges trust in ourselves for a steadfast and abiding trust in God's goodness and willingness to respond. The heavenly Father whom Jesus revealed to us is not reluctant to act on our behalf. God is not an unyielding boulder against which prayer must come repeatedly like the blow of a sledgehammer. True persistence arises as we come to see that our goal is not to overcome God's resistance but to release God's willingness. Believing this about God leads us to be diligent in prayer. When we know that God will act in God's own good time, we can pray in faith until the answer comes.

In the meantime, the attitude of persistence evokes from us active rather than passive faith. It leads to the kind of trust in God that is characterized by wholehearted engagement in the Lord's work even as we "wait upon the Lord" to answer our petitions. In one of her writings, Ethel Barrett relates the story of a handicapped boy, Steve Paxon, which illustrates this kind of active faith:

> Steve prayed that God would take away his stammer when he was a little boy. When he was a man, he still stammered. But he hadn't spent his time moping in the meanwhile. He'd taught himself to read, to sing, and had established himself in a profitable business. When he started his Sunday School ministry he asked God again to take away the stammer. But it was four long years before he discovered that by breathing a certain way he finally had it conquered!
>
> That was a long time to wait for a prayer to be answered. But while Steve was waiting, he was too busy to sulk. . . . The long years of waiting had tested his mettle, rubbed off the sharp edges in his personality, taught him patience, so that when the answer came he was ready for it.
>
> As fascinating as Steve Paxon's whole story is, the most amazing part comes at the very end. For after his great missionary work was established and others were able to take his place in the field, his job was to travel back east to Boston, New York, Philadelphia — all the key cities and, of all things — speak! Yes, his final mission in life was to be a speaker! In the end, his speaking ability was his greatest strength.[5]

5. Barrett, *Sometimes I Feel Like a Blob* (Glendale, Calif.: Regal Books, 1965), pp. 67-70.

While he was on earth, Jesus taught the importance of persistent prayer: "Then Jesus told his disciples a parable to show them that they should always pray and not give up" (Luke 18:1). The risen Lord desires that we persist in prayer as well. And he admonishes us never to give up but continually to cry for the kingdom. Like his first-century disciples, we too are invited to come before the Sovereign God, the One who reigns over the universe, with the petition "Your kingdom come, your will be done on earth as it is in heaven." Our Lord has promised that his heavenly Father honors such prayer. God will respond, both in the situations that we face in the present and, above all, on that glorious day when the kingdom comes in its fullness.

6. Practicing Effective Prayer

Prayer is not merely voicing the occasional petition to God. Nor is it badgering God in the vain hope of getting him to do what *we* want. Rather, prayer is an ongoing conversation with God. The purpose of this conversation is to discover the divine will so that we can effectively cry for the kingdom. As a consequence, in prayer we petition the Sovereign God of the universe who is our loving heavenly Father with the cry "Your kingdom come, your will be done on earth as it is in heaven." In prayer, we continually and persistently invoke the in-breaking of the kingdom into the circumstances of the present.

But when, or with whom, should we engage in this practice?

In this final chapter, I want to respond to this question by suggesting how we can pray effectively in the three central settings of our individual and communal journeys. I want to explore the manner in which we ought to pray when we gather in public worship, when we pray alone, and when we come together in prayer groups.

Let me preface my remarks by noting that Scripture provides a basis for praying in each of these three settings. According to the Bible, we are to give prayer a prominent place in public worship. Paul instructed Timothy regarding the public gathering, "I urge, then, first of all, that requests, prayers, intercession and thanksgiving be made for everyone" (1 Tim. 2:1). He then added, "I want men everywhere to lift up holy hands in prayer, without anger or disputing" (1 Tim. 2:8).

Moreover, when we meet in smaller groups to pray, we can claim the promise that our Lord is present. Jesus said, "Again, I tell you that if two of you on earth agree about anything you ask for, it will be done for you by my Father in heaven. For where two or three come together in my name, there am I with them" (Matt. 18:19-20). Although our Lord initially spoke these words in the context of church discipline, the principle he articulated is readily applicable to us when we meet together for prayer.

Likewise, the practice of praying alone finds its basis in a host of biblical examples, including in the lives of Jesus and the apostles. As I noted in Chapter One, the Gospels emphasize that Jesus was a man of prayer who repeatedly went away from the crowds to be alone with his Father (Matt. 6:6; 14:23; Luke 6:12). The apostle Paul followed in the footsteps of Jesus, for his practice was to "kneel before the Father" in prayer (e.g., Eph. 3:14-16).

I should note as well that these activities are not wholly distinct from each other. Prayer that occurs in solitude reaches outward to the communal prayer that we share together.[1] At the same time, our participation together in communal prayer lays the foundation for the praying that we do alone. Indeed, even in the solitude of our private "prayer chamber" we continue to say "*Our* Father."

This interrelationship may be viewed in another way as well. The prayer that I offer in solitude dare not be merely my "private" prayer. It should never be a matter solely of my own concern. Instead, my prayer ought to reach out to others as well. In the solitude of my "prayer chamber" I ought to be serving the needs of others as I lift them before the One who is "Our Father." And as I say "*Our* Father" in prayer, I am reminded that even my personal needs, when lifted to the throne of grace, become by that act the concern of the community of all those who address God in this manner. Eugene H. Peterson offers a helpful description of the distinction between solitude and privacy: "Privacy is our attempt to insulate the self from interference; solitude leaves the company of others for a time in order to listen to them more deeply, be aware of them, serve them."[2]

In a similar manner, our communal prayers do not merely bring before God the "big" issues that affect the world, the global church, or even our congregation as a whole. They also include the needs of indi-

---

1. George A. Buttrick, *The Power of Prayer Today* (Waco, Tex.: Word Books, 1970), p. 248.

2. Peterson, *Earth and Altar: The Community of Prayer in a Self-Bound Society* (Downers Grove, Ill.: InterVarsity Press, 1985), p. 16.

vidual persons. And even as they bring to God matters that affect us all, they include "me" within their scope.

All prayer, therefore, is both personal and communal. Whenever you or I pray, we are always addressing God as those who are members of the people who belong to God through Jesus Christ. Sometimes my petitions center on my own needs and concerns; at other times, my prayers focus on other people. Yet in each case, I ought to be profoundly aware that I pray as one who participates in a people. This awareness, in turn, ought to cause me to remember that I am in fact voicing all of my petitions on behalf of the whole.

Praying in Public Worship

The ultimate expression of prayer, the ultimate cry for the kingdom, is worship. Worship is the celebration in the here-and-now of the future kingdom of God. In the present, we experience only glimpses of the in-breaking kingdom. Yet in the midst of the evil, suffering, and trials that come our way, we remain a people of hope. We believe that God's rule, which will be present in its fullness one glorious future day, is already dawning. Worship is the festive foretaste of the future kingdom.

It is not surprising, then, that prayer is to have a significant place in our worship celebrations. Moreover, the cry "Your kingdom come, your will be done on earth as it is in heaven," voiced in prayer closets and in prayer groups, is actually an extension of the communal prayer of the gathered people.

One important vehicle for practicing effective prayer in the worship service is the public prayers that are spoken. When we pray publicly, we do so because we have been delegated by the gathered congregation to voice to God the prayers of the people as a whole. This means that whoever is given the great privilege and responsibility to pray in the assembly has the task of expressing audibly the heartfelt prayers of the gathered community.

I recall how in the Baptist churches that my father served folks would speak about one or another member being called on to "lead in prayer." This cliché is actually a fitting description of public prayer, for the one who prays in public is indeed a prayer leader. He or she has the task of *leading* the congregation in the time of prayer.

Furthermore, in many churches, the congregation routinely voices an "Amen" at the close of every public prayer. This too reflects an important dimension of communal prayer. It indicates that the gathered people are in agreement with the spoken prayer and that this prayer has gathered together into a single whole their unspoken prayers. The "Amen" indicates that the audible prayer has truly become the prayer of the people.

1. Suggestions to the One Who Prays Publicly

On the basis of this understanding of the nature of public prayer, let me offer a few suggestions for those who are asked to lead the congregation in prayer that can assist in making this practice effective.

First, be sensitive to the leading of the Spirit. This sensitivity arises out of a profound understanding of, and a deep appreciation for, your role as the one who is carrying the prayers of the gathered community to God. Keep in mind that the Spirit is the One who has drawn God's people to prayer. Your role, in turn, is to seek the mind of the Spirit so that you are able to articulate and lift to God the prayers of the people. You are voicing in an audible manner their inaudible prayers.

For this reason, I find it preferable to speak in the plural — "we," "our" — rather than in the singular — "I," "my." Although the *words* that you pray are yours, the *prayer* that you offer is in fact that of the entire community. This also means that you should not focus your prayer on your own personal requests, needs, and concerns. Instead, your prayer should bring to God the supplications that are shared among the people who have gathered to worship.

Second, remember that the prayer is being addressed to God by a representative of the people and not to the people by a representative of God. Your role is not that of telling the listeners what you think God wants them to hear, but to voice the prayers of the community to God. Public prayer, therefore, is not an opportunity to preach to or to evangelize the audience. Nor should it be used to voice your disapproval of someone in the gathered community.

LeRoy Patterson describes several ways in which public prayer is mistakenly used to speak to the audience rather than to God. One such prayer is "the holy promotion," in which prayer is used to raise support for a pet project or to announce a coming attraction. In "the lecture prayer," prayer becomes a pretense "for clubbing the sheep into line." "The summary prayer" is offered at the end of the service, when the preacher "feels obligated to summarize the message he has just preached, even to reiterate the three main points in case someone missed them."[3] In contrast to these "mistakes," prayer must always be addressed to God, never to others. Therefore, avoid the temptation to pray "for the benefit of" those who are silently listening.

Third, let the four elements of prayer delineated in the ACTS acrostic guide you. Well-planned worship services often follow the basic ACTS progression. When this is the case, the location of your prayer within the overall structure of the service determines which of the four elements should be the focus of your prayer. Often the main public prayer comes at the point in the service when the petitions of the people are to be lifted to God. At this point, the congregation has already engaged in adoration, confession, and thanksgiving. In this case, your prayer can simply omit these three elements and move directly to supplication.

Fourth, be sensitive to prayer content, length, and volume. Although each public prayer is voiced by one particular person, in fact the entire people are to be involved. For this reason, a prayer that is too lengthy or too personal (i.e., that focuses on the pray-er) will be ineffective, for it may be unable to bring the congregation along with it. Likewise, praying either too loudly or too quietly can hinder the people from joining in the experience.

Finally, live in a manner that is worthy of the honor of praying in public. Paul describes public prayer as the raising of "holy hands" (1 Tim. 2:8). Only those whose lives are pleasing to God can truly lift holy hands in the assembly of believers.[4]

---

3. Patterson, "The Ten Most Unwanted Public Prayer Habits," *Eternity*, October 1982, pp. 35-36.

4. The role of prayer in the life of the pastor, who often is the one who voices the public prayer, has not been singled out for discussion here. For a discussion of this topic, see E. M. Bounds, *The Weapon of Prayer* (Chicago: Moody, 1980), pp. 111-13; and Steve Harper, *Prayer Ministry in the Local Church* (Grand Rapids: Baker, 1976), p. 28.

2. Suggestions for the Congregation

During times of public prayer, the congregation has a vital role to play as well. We who are gathered for worship are not to be mere passive observers but actual participants in this act of worship. Following several important suggestions will assist us in doing our part in making this practice of prayer effective.

First, we should assume a reverent attitude when someone begins to pray. Public prayer is a holy moment, not only for the prayer leader but also for each of us who are present. Actually, public prayer offers an opportunity for true congregational prayer, a prayer in which each worshiper is to be actively engaged. As in every situation of prayer, our active participation begins with a reverent attitude.

Second, we should seek to be conscious of the nearness of God during the time of prayer. Prayer is a drawing near to God. And this ought to be the case not only for the prayer leader but also for all who have gathered for worship. Our thoughts, therefore, ought to be turned heavenward, so that we might be able to sense the presence of God in this time of conversation.

Third, we should listen to the prayer sympathetically as those who are standing with the pray-er before God in prayer. Sympathetic listening begins as we become sensitive to the purpose of public prayer — namely, to gather our prayers together and voice our communal prayer to God. The pray-er, in short, is praying on our behalf.

Fourth, we should take ownership of, personalize, or take to ourselves the prayer being voiced. Making the prayer our own requires that we pay attention to what is being said. As we listen, we are enabled to offer our personal agreement with the prayer. This agreement may at times be verbalized by means of semi-audible responses (e.g., "Yes, Lord!") during the prayer or an "Amen" at the end. We must do so consciously and honestly, however, lest our interjection of such expressions of agreement degenerate into mere force of habit. Likewise, the responses that we voice during the prayer should not be so audible or so frequent that they disturb the reverent mood or disrupt the concentration of others.

Fifth, we should listen for the voice of the Spirit during the prayer. Because public prayer is a time of conversation involving God and the gathered community, we can enter into prayer expecting him to communicate with us.

Finally, we should allow this occasion to become a basis for celebration. The kingdom of God is coming in its fullness. We have gathered to celebrate this hope as well as the foretastes of the kingdom that we are enjoying in the present. For this reason, even the cry for the kingdom voiced on behalf of God's people is celebratory, for we pray confident that God will hear this cry.

Praying Alone

For most Christians, the vast majority of prayer occurs alone. Sometimes we pray alone in our private "prayer closet." At other times, we recede into the "private chamber" of our own hearts, even though we are in a public place. This private chamber is a crucial setting for the practice of prayer. In fact, many of the answers that we receive to prayer come in response to personal prayer. Praying alone, therefore, can revolutionize our own lives and affect greatly the lives of others.

The role of praying alone in the evangelization of the world has been emphasized by various missionary enterprises. For several decades, Every Home for Christ (formerly the World Literature Crusade) has attempted to enlist a host of "one-hour watchers," a group of Christians who are willing to spend one hour a day alone in prayer. In this manner, these believers provide a necessary dimension of support to the worldwide missionary enterprise.

1. The Basic Aspects of Praying Alone

Well-rounded personal prayer includes three basic activities: meditation, verbalized prayer, and silence.

Christian meditation is prayerful reflection on the word of God.[5] In meditation, we turn a Scripture text over in our mind with the goal of being taught by the Spirit how we should apply this word from God to our own personal lives. Through meditation on the Word, we can come to understand what the Spirit is saying to us and to the church, as we seek to be the people of God in the context in which God has placed us.

5. See Norman Pittenger, *Praying Today* (Grand Rapids: Eerdmans, 1974), pp. 60-61.

In verbalizing our prayers to God, we are seeking to commune with and to communicate with God. In general, when we pray we ought to follow the ACTS format: adoration, confession, thanksgiving, and supplication. Of course, not every prayer that we voice will include all four aspects. But over the course of time we should be giving place to each of the four. Our verbalized prayer ought also to be "Word-enriched," as we draw from the Scriptures the basis for what we pray. Praying the Scriptures causes prayer to come to life. And it is an important key to offering petitions that are in accordance with God's will.

Silence can also be an important aspect of praying alone. Because prayer is a two-way conversation, we naturally want to give space for God to speak. Silence, therefore, is not necessarily passive, but rather entails active listening for the voice of God. Andrew Murray, a great prayer warrior of a previous generation, offered this helpful advice:

> And when you are praying, let there be intervals of silence, reverent stillness of soul, in which you yield yourself to God, in case He may have aught He wishes to teach you or to work in you. Waiting on Him will become the most blessed part of prayer, and the blessing thus obtained will be doubly precious as the fruit of such fellowship with the Holy One.[6]

2. The Daily Devotional Habit

Crucial to the ongoing experience of personal prayer is the development of a daily time of personal devotions. This daily devotional time facilitates spiritual growth. And it can become a vital component in our ongoing attempt to walk in the Spirit.

When in the course of the day should we engage in this practice of daily prayer? If we look at the lives of the saints given in the Scriptures, we find several models.

Some persons practiced the discipline of praying three times each day. In fact, this seems to have been a standard practice among the Hebrews. While in exile in Babylon, Daniel followed this practice (Dan. 6:10). Likewise, the psalmist declared, "But I call to God, and the LORD

---

6. Andrew Murray, *Waiting on God* (London: Oliphants, 1961), p. 25.

saves me. Evening, morning and noon I cry out in distress, and he hears my voice" (Ps. 55:16-17). Peter may have followed this Old Testament model as well. In any case, he definitely prayed each day at noon. In fact, when the envoys from Cornelius arrived, the apostle was engaging in noon-hour prayer (Acts 10:9).

Perhaps the most significant practice that we find in Scripture, however, is the discipline of devoting the early moments of the morning to prayer. The psalmist writes, "Morning by morning, O LORD, you hear my voice; morning by morning I lay my requests before you and wait in expectation" (Ps. 5:3). Jesus followed the practice of morning prayer: "Very early in the morning, while it was still dark, Jesus got up, left the house and went off to a solitary place, where he prayed" (Mark 1:35).

I would urge you to develop the daily practice of personal prayer, if you have not already done so. Of course, you will need to decide for yourself what time of day works best for you. And this will be based on your own needs, schedules, and daily routine. Yet I would suggest that, when possible, the ideal time for personal prayer is in the morning. Beginning the day with prayer has a great advantage because it allows us to start the day with the Lord in a deliberate and conscious manner. To facilitate the goal of "starting the day with the Lord," let me outline a five-step pattern for a personal morning devotional time.

First, having come away from the world — the telephone, other people, and so forth — and having entered into the closet of prayer, begin the time of solitude with a short prayer. In this prayer, invoke the presence of the Holy Spirit during your devotional time. And invite the Spirit to illumine the Scriptures and to prompt you to pray in accordance with God's will.

Second, open the Bible to the reading that you have selected for the day. Study the text and meditate on God's Word.

Third, prepare to enter into the presence of the God of the universe.[7] To do so, review the requests that you intend to bring before God's throne of grace and give some thought to how you will structure your time of prayer. You may find a journal or prayer notebook containing your ongoing prayer requests to be of assistance. In addition, seek to discern the crucial prayer need of the day. On some days, you

---

7. For a refutation of objections to such planned prayer, see Stephen F. Winward, *Teach Yourself to Pray* (New York: Harper & Brothers, 1961), p. 39.

may sense that your prayer should center on adoration, praising God for his glorious character. On other days, you may find that confession or thanksgiving is the priority. And there will be days when all you can do is pour out your heart in supplication. Seek to determine, therefore, whether you are being moved to focus on one or another of these dimensions of prayer or whether following the general ACTS format is more appropriate.

Fourth, pray.

Before you leave the prayer chamber, there is one final exercise that I would urge you to complete: visualize the day with God. Spend a few moments looking ahead to the events and opportunities of the day. As you name these events, picture how God will be present in each one. For example, for most of us, the routine of life brings certain predictable temptations. Therefore, visualize how God will provide strength and victory to you today as you face this daily onslaught. In addition, each day generally brings similar opportunities for witness, service, and ministry. Name these, and visualize how the Holy Spirit will provide the strength you need to be salt and light during the coming day.

Once you have finished this fifth exercise, you are ready to face the day armed with the resources of God. As the day unfolds, becoming yet another opportunity to walk with the Spirit and to experience the joy of the Lord even in the midst of the brokenness and evil that you encounter, you will discover that praying alone has once again been an effective practice.

3. Further Suggestions

Let me round out this section by offering a few additional suggestions for facilitating an effective personal prayer life.

First, I would reiterate the idea of a prayer notebook (or a prayer spreadsheet on your computer) which contains a section devoted to supplication. Divide each page in this section into four columns. In the first two, note the date and the description of each prayer request for which you come to be burdened. Then, as each situation is resolved, note in columns three and four the date and the manner in which the answer to the request came. In this way, the prayer notebook can become a record not only of your requests but also of God's answers.

Later, when you are tempted to stop praying, a quick review of the note-book will remind you how effective praying alone has been in the past. And this review will encourage you to remain faithful in crying for the kingdom.

Second, I would also remind you of the technique of using "faith-sized requests" that I mentioned in Chapter Four. Faith-sized requests can help you "climb the steps" toward receiving God's answer to a complex and complicated circumstance. Record in your prayer notebook how you are dividing large petitions into faith-sized requests. And don't forget to add God's answers to each of these smaller petitions as they come.

Third, read devotional literature. I would include under this heading the prayers in the Bible, which can become helpful models for us as we seek to pray effectively. In addition, devotional booklets provide an ongoing resource of new material for thoughtful reflection and prayer. You might also find great help in books containing the prayers of great Christians. Books about prayer can deepen your own understanding of what makes for effective praying. And autobiographies of great Christians can help motivate you to pray faithfully.

Fourth, be cognizant that your personal devotions are a time of worship. Realize that not only prayer but also Bible study can be offered to God as an act of worship. You could consider adding actual acts of worship, such as singing to God, to your daily devotions.

Fifth, pray semi-audibly. This might help you to keep your mind from wandering.

Sixth, be conscious of the One whom you are addressing in prayer. You are in the presence of the God who is Person in the highest sense, so relate to God person to person. God is likewise triune. Therefore, be conscience of the role of each Trinitarian member in the act of prayer. Ultimately, the work of the Holy Spirit is to draw us into the relationship that the Son enjoys with the Father. And prayer is one aspect of this dynamic of participation. As I noted in Chapter Four, we can address each of the three in accordance with the nature of the prayer we are voicing.

Finally, keep in mind that the most crucial point in personal prayer is to do it. Aspects such as content, format, time of day, and so on are important, of course. Yet they are all secondary to regular, consistent praying. Seek therefore to develop the habit of praying alone. The key to making prayer a regular part of life lies with your will. Thus, ask continually, "Do I see prayer as being so crucial that I am willing to pay the price necessary to become the person of prayer God wants me to be?" E. Stanley Jones offered an illustration of the drastic measure that one person took so that he might learn to pray:

> A great Christian in England was very sleepy-headed as a youth, and no matter how much he resolved, he slept past his prayer time. He decided on desperate measures — as penalty he would throw a guinea into the river every time he missed his prayer time. He did this for several mornings and sadly paid the penalty — a heavy one for a poor student. But at last the mind responded, the prayer habit was fixed, and he became one of the outstanding spiritual men of his generation.[8]

Praying Together

In addition to participating in communal acts of prayer and praying alone, we can practice effective praying by banding together with other believers in prayer groups. Praying together is another way of giving expression to the awareness that we belong to each other that we voice each time we say, "Our Father."[9] In addition, participating in a prayer group offers several benefits that may not be present in praying alone.[10]

1. Benefits of Group Prayer

As I noted earlier in this chapter, coming together as a small group allows us to claim a special promise of Christ's presence (Matt. 18:19-20). Praying in groups also helps us share each other's burdens. Paul encouraged the Galatians, "Carry each other's burdens, and in this way you will fulfill the law of Christ" (Gal. 6:2). Praying for others within the context of a prayer group is an effective means of carrying out this admonition.

8. Jones, *Victorious Living* (London: Hodder & Stoughton, 1936), p. 68.

9. For a discussion of how prayer groups can be developed in a congregation, see Steve Harper, *Prayer Ministry in the Local Church* (Grand Rapids: Baker, 1976), pp. 47-56.

10. See Rosalind Rinker, *Prayer: Conversing with God* (Grand Rapids: Zondervan, 1959), pp. 44-45.

Furthermore, praying together strengthens our resolve to face boldly life's difficulties. When we are with others, we realize anew that we do not stand alone. Each of us is encouraged by the faith of the others. And we are all supported by the intercessory prayers of the group.

Another glorious benefit that can come by praying together is the discovery of God's will. Indeed, often God reveals his will to Christians who have banded together to pray rather than to a believer praying alone. The intention of the Holy Spirit to send Paul and Barnabas into the missionary enterprise was revealed in just this way. Luke reports that it was "while they were worshiping the Lord and fasting" that the Holy Spirit called upon the praying community to set apart these two emissaries for the missionary enterprise (Acts 13:1-3).

Several years ago I experienced this benefit firsthand while serving as interim pastor of a congregation in the Midwest. In September of that year, John, a faithful member of the church, found out that his position at the local hospital was being eliminated. Realizing that the search for a new position would require that the family move to another part of the country, John and his wife, Mary, immediately put their house on the market. When John had prospects for a job but no buyer in sight, I suggested to him that what their situation needed was a "good, old-fashioned cottage prayer meeting." At first, he was cool to the idea. In March, however, John concluded that the time was right for such a meeting.

I called a small group of trusted friends, who on the appointed evening gathered in John and Mary's living room. Within ten minutes we had gone around the circle, each person having voiced in turn the same basic prayer: "Find John a job, and please bring a buyer for their house, if it be your will." Our task completed, everyone waited for me to offer the final prayer. But I was convinced that God had more in store for us that evening. So rather than ending the prayer session, I waited. During what seemed to everyone present to be a long and uncomfortable silence that followed, I sensed that I was to claim in prayer that the house would be sold by the end of the school year. At first, I resisted the urge. Finally, however, I gave in, voicing — albeit reluctantly — the prayer that I sensed the Spirit was commanding me to speak. To my surprise, my prayer was immediately echoed by a second person in the group. "Father," I said inaudibly, "the biblical principle is that truth is established by the testimony of two or three witnesses. If we have discerned your will, let there be a third witness." Almost immediately, a third voice echoed our claim.

Soon after this prayer meeting, John accepted a position in California. Two days before the end of the school year, his family's house sold. By praying together in that small group that night, we had discerned the will of God!

Finally, as this incident also indicates, praying together deepens our relationship to each other. As we share our heartfelt concerns with one another in prayer, and as we experience together the struggles and joys that group prayer brings, we discover that the Spirit is forging a special bond among us.

2. Types of Group Prayer

Most times of group prayer follow one of two basic approaches. The first is what we might call "circle prayer." In circle prayer each participant voices a complete prayer before the next person begins. Generally each person prays only once and voices all of his or her praises, thanksgivings, and requests during that one prayer. And circle prayer is person-centered; one person prays, and the others listen.

In the second approach, "conversational prayer," each participant prays only a few sentences at a time, voicing at that moment an incomplete prayer or only part of a prayer. Each participant may pray several times. But he or she mentions only one item on each occasion. This type of prayer is topic-centered, in that the prayer of the group moves from topic to topic. Everyone focuses on one particular topic until all have had the opportunity to join in praying about it. Only then is another topic introduced.

Each of these basic types of prayer has advantages. Because circle prayer is more familiar to most people, it might be less threatening for some. Under several circumstances it is preferable to conversational prayer. In large group meetings, for example, it facilitates the participation of many people in prayer. Circle prayer is also preferable when the group members do not know one another well, in that participants in circle prayer are not required to be as sensitive to the mood or spirit of the group. And circle prayer is preferable when sufficient time for conversational prayer is not available.

Conversational prayer also has certain advantages. For example, it allows for greater depth in prayer. Unlike what often happens in circle prayer, in conversational prayer the participants do not find themselves repeating the same general, basic request that others have already mentioned. As a consequence, the group is enabled to move beyond the level of general petition and delve into the deeper and more particular aspects of the need that they are bringing to God.

More so than circle prayer, conversational prayer aids the group in the task of discerning God's will and seeing God's answer. By proceeding topically, the entire group is able to concentrate on the specific request at hand. The group focus, when coupled with periods of silence, allows the participants to listen for God's voice and to seek single-mindedly the mind of God.

Conversational prayer also provides an occasion for participants who come with deep burdens to receive an immediate spiritual boost. Those who interject, even in a halting fashion, a personal request find themselves immediately supported in prayer by the group. This immediate response brings immediate encouragement. Similarly, conversational prayer may be less threatening for new Christians or bashful pray-ers. Indeed, no one is required to be able to voice a lengthy, eloquent prayer to participate in conversational prayer.

Finally, it is generally easier to concentrate on the prayer being voiced in conversational prayer than in circle prayer. Participants in circle prayer often find themselves tempted to plan what they intend to say, even while they are listening to the lengthy prayer of another. In conversational prayer, in contrast, each participant can focus on the one request regarding which all are at this point praying.

Prayer groups that practice conversational prayer can be a great asset to the church of Jesus Christ.

3. The Practice of Conversational Prayer

If our times of conversational prayer are to be effective, we must be properly motivated. We must desire to be sensitive to the promptings of the Spirit, and we must seek to avoid quenching the moving of the Holy Spirit within the group.

Likewise, we must be motivated to create a climate of freedom in prayer, so that each participant can be open and responsive to the Spirit's promptings. In conversational prayer, no one must feel forced to pray. Rather, each person must be granted the privilege of not praying without feeling guilty.

Because it is in an important sense genuine conversation, conversational prayer shares certain characteristics present in all human conversation.[11] Prayer entails conversing with God, of course. Therefore, in our times of conversational prayer, we might want to visualize the presence of God at the center of the group.

Just as in a normal conversation with others, in conversational prayer we will need to be topic-oriented rather than individual-oriented. This topic focus includes being willing to "pray through" situations and requests as a group and to aid one another in prayer as specific issues are voiced. In conversational prayer, the length of the individual prayers is not as crucial as the fact that each "mini-prayer" addresses only the topic at hand. When a specific topic is introduced, we should allow all who want to pray about it to do so before moving on to a different subject. We ought to wait for one another before introducing a new topic.

In conversational prayer, silence will be a repeated experience, as we give place for the unhurried movement of the Spirit. One of the major obstacles in this kind of praying is the nervousness that some may sense during times of silence. Yet silence is valuable in conversational prayer because it allows the Spirit to speak.

Finally, in conversational prayer we must pray honestly and in a straightforward manner. Rosalind Rinker correctly outlines a twofold principle of honesty:

> First, that I say *I* when I mean myself, and that I say *we* when I include the whole group. The editorial *we* denotes the deadly poison of dishonesty. . . .
>
> The second principle of honesty is to pray where I am and not where I am not.[12]

Quite obviously, the type of honesty that refuses to pray as if one's life is totally in order when in fact it is in disarray requires a deep level of

---

11. Rinker, *Prayer*, pp. 23-24.
12. Rinker, *Prayer*, pp. 87-88.

trust within the group. Nevertheless, it is this depth of relationship that releases conversational prayer to be a vital, healing, and effective activity.

Group prayer, whether circle or conversational, is a natural extension of the personal life of prayer. It is called forth by personal prayer and in turn fosters it. At the same time, group prayer is dependent on and enhances the communal prayer of the gathered community.

Epilogue: The Life of Prayer

Our journey of discovery into the working of prayer has now come to an end. In these pages we have explored how prayer is the cry for the kingdom. We have discovered that prayer is not merely petitioning God for a grab bag of miscellaneous items on a spiritual wish list. Rather, in prayer we invoke the coming of the kingdom of God into the circumstances that we are facing, even as we petition our loving heavenly Father to bring the divine program for history to its completion in the return of our Lord. In the various situations of life, we cry out to God, "Your will be done on earth as it is in heaven." As in this manner we pray according to God's will, we discover that we are laying hold of God's willingness and ability to act. As a consequence, we are able to pray confidently and persistently. And we do so within the public worship of the community, in the privacy of our own "prayer chamber," and in groups of praying Christians.

Our journey of discovery has netted these insights into the dynamic of prayer. Although the intellectual journey that we launched at the beginning of the book has reached its end, the journey of discovering the work of prayer is never-ending. This pilgrimage is a lifelong journey. For this reason, our goal ought to be that of allowing prayer to be a lifelong pursuit. My life, your life, and our life together ought to become a life of prayer.

Because the life of prayer is significant, we ought never to treat prayer lightly. But how can we accomplish this? How can we enter into a life of prayer?

I would suggest that we can be launched into the life of prayer as we seek to be continually conscious of the needs of others. To do so, however, requires that we engage in sympathetic listening. In conversations with others, we may need to read between the lines so that we can hear the real but hidden needs that others are attempting to express to us. We then take these needs to God in prayer. And rather than criticizing others, we will be quick to pray for them, even for our enemies.

Launching into a life of effective prayer likewise requires that we be continually conscious of prayer, so that prayer becomes a part of our entire life. I believe that Paul may have had this in mind when he admonished his readers, "Pray without ceasing" (1 Thess. 5:17, KJV). Paul is not suggesting that we should spend each moment of the day alone in our "prayer closet." Rather, he is urging us to be bathed continuously with the awareness of God's presence and to respond to this awareness not only by living in a prayerful manner but by making all of life a conversation with God.

This means that we can pray during routine tasks. We can pray whether we are in the shower, in the subway, or in the shopping center. And when the name of someone comes to mind, we should assume that the Holy Spirit is prompting us to pray for this person. The same experience may occur in the middle of the night. If we are awakened from sleep, we need to consider the possibility that the Spirit is summoning us to prayer.

One such summons occurred one Sunday night in April 1912. That night the *Titanic* was struck by an iceberg. Colonel Gracy, a passenger on the ship, after helping launch the few lifeboats that were available, resigned himself to death. As he slipped beneath the waves, his wife at home was suddenly awakened, her mind filled with great concern for her husband. She prayed for several hours, until peace came into her heart. Meanwhile, the Colonel had bobbed to the surface near a capsized boat and eventually was rescued. He and his wife later discovered that during the very hours she was agonizing in prayer, he was clinging desperately to this overturned craft.

To develop a life of prayer requires as well that we cultivate in prayer a relationship with the triune God. Rather than repeatedly addressing prayer to "God," we should develop a consciousness of communing with each member of the Trinity.

A life of prayer emerges likewise when we realize that God is concerned with all aspects of life. Nothing is too big or too small for him. So often when we try to discern God at work in our world, we look to dramatic or miraculous events. Although God does intervene directly in our world, answers to prayer do not always come in dramatic and miraculous ways. God is also at work in natural processes. Prayer can release us to see this, insofar as prayer transforms our own attitude and outlook. Through prayer, we can catch a sense of the awesome and awe-inspiring presence of God even within the mundane, natural flow of life. If we would pray well, we must be open to being transformed in this manner.

Ultimately, however, the only way to develop a life of prayer is by praying. After the books have been read and the principles have been understood, we are left with the task of launching out into the unknown. It is there, however, that God waits, beckoning us to embark on the exciting adventure of prayer — beckoning us, in short, to cry for the kingdom. For prayer is one significant means whereby we become partners with God in bringing the kingdom of God, which is the future of the world, into the circumstances of life in the present.

The greatest challenge that we face today is the challenge to pray. Meeting this challenge requires that we cease merely talking about prayer and begin to pray. Karl Rahner aptly concluded, "What we can say *about* prayer is of little consequence: what matters is what we say *in* prayer."[1]

Let us, therefore, pray. Let us invoke the in-breaking of the kingdom into the situations of life that we face. Let us cry for the kingdom!

---

1. Rahner, *On Prayer* (New York: Paulist, 1968), pp. 108-9.

Selected Bibliography

Books about Prayer

Austin, Bill. *The Back of God.* Wheaton, Ill.: Tyndale House, 1980.

Baelz, Peter. *Does God Answer Prayer?* London: Darton, Longman & Todd, 1982.

———. *Prayer and Providence.* New York: Seabury Press, 1968.

Barth, Karl. *Prayer.* Philadelphia: Westminster, 1985.

Bauman, Edward W. *Intercessory Prayer.* Philadelphia: Westminster, 1958.

Belden, Albert D. *The Practice of Prayer.* New York: Harper & Brothers, n.d.

Biederwolf, William Edward. *How Can God Answer Prayer?* 2d ed. Grand Rapids: Eerdmans, 1937.

Biersdorf, John E. *Healing of Purpose.* Nashville: Abingdon, 1985.

Billheimer, Paul E. *Destined for the Throne.* Fort Washington, Pa.: Christian Literature Crusade, 1975.

Blackwood, Andrew W. *Leading in Public Prayer.* New York: Abingdon, 1958.

Bloesch, Donald G. *The Struggle of Prayer.* San Francisco: Harper & Row, 1980.

Bloom, Anthony. *Beginning to Pray.* New York: Paulist, 1970.

———. *Courage to Pray.* New York: Paulist, 1973.

———. *Living Prayer.* Springfield, Ill.: Templegate, 1966.

Boulding, Maria. *Prayer: Our Journey Home.* Ann Arbor, Mich.: Servant Books, 1980.

Bounds, E. M. *The Essentials of Prayer.* New York: Revell, 1925.

———. *The Possibilities of Prayer.* Chicago: Moody, 1980.

———. *Purpose in Prayer.* London: Marshall Brothers, n.d.

———. *The Reality of Prayer.* Chicago: Moody, 1980.

———. *The Weapon of Prayer.* Chicago: Moody, 1980.

Bowdon, Boyce A. *Empowered: Living Experiences of Talking with God.* Atlanta: John Knox, 1978.

Brümmer, Vincent. *What Are We Doing When We Pray? A Philosophical Inquiry.* London: SCM, 1984.

Bunyan, John. *Prayer.* London: Banner of Truth Trust, 1962.

Buttrick, George A. *The Power of Prayer Today.* Waco, Tex.: Word Books, 1970.

————. *Prayer.* New York: Abingdon-Cokesbury Press, 1942.

Carse, James P. *The Silence of God.* New York: Macmillan, 1985.

Casteel, John L. *Rediscovering Prayer.* New York: Association Press, 1955.

Caulfield, Sean. *The Experience of Praying.* New York: Paulist, 1980.

Chadwick, Samuel. *The Path of Prayer.* London: Hodder & Stoughton, 1931.

Change the World School of Prayer Manual. 2d ed. Studio City, Calif.: World Literature Crusade, 1978.

Coggan, Donald. *The Prayers of the New Testament.* London: Hodder & Stoughton, 1967.

Constable, Thomas L. *Talking to God: What the Bible Says about Prayer.* Grand Rapids: Baker, 1995.

Crosby, Michael H. *Thy Will Be Done.* Maryknoll, N.Y.: Orbis Books, 1977.

Daly, Gabriel. *Asking the Father.* Wilmington, Del.: Michael Glazier, 1982.

Dobson, Theodore. *How to Pray for Spiritual Growth.* New York: Paulist, 1982.

Doty, William L. *Prayer in the Spirit.* Staten Island, N.Y.: Alba House, 1973.

Dubay, Thomas. *Pilgrims Pray.* New York: Alba House, 1974.

Eastman, Dick. *The Hour That Changes the World.* Grand Rapids: Baker, 1978.

Ebeling, Gerhard. *On Prayer.* Philadelphia: Fortress, 1966.

Ellul, Jacques. *Prayer and Modern Man.* New York: Seabury Press, 1970.

Emery, Pierre-Yves. *Prayer at the Heart of Life.* Maryknoll, N.Y.: Orbis Books, 1975.

Fisher, Fred L. *Prayer in the New Testament.* Philadelphia: Westminster, 1964.

Forrester, David. *Listening with the Heart.* New York: Paulist, 1978.

Forsyth, P. T. *The Soul of Prayer.* 1916; London: Independent Press, 1960.

Fosdick, Harry Emerson. *The Meaning of Prayer.* New York: Association Press, 1915.

Foster, Richard. *Prayer: Finding the Heart's True Home.* San Francisco: Harper San Francisco, 1992.

Friedman, Greg. *It Begins with Friendship.* Cincinnati, Ohio: St. Anthony Messenger Press, 1984.

Giardini, P. Fabio. *Loving Awareness of God's Presence in Prayer.* New York: Alba House, 1978.

Gordon, S. D. *Quiet Talks on Prayer.* London: Revell, n.d.

Green, Thomas H. *When the Well Runs Dry.* Notre Dame, Ind.: Ave Maria Press, 1979.

Griffin, Emilie. *Clinging: The Experience of Prayer.* San Francisco: Harper & Row, 1984.

Griffiss, James E. *A Silent Path to God*. Philadelphia: Fortress, 1980.

Guenther, Margaret. *The Practice of Prayer*. Toronto: Anglican Book Centre, 1998.

Hallesby, O. *Prayer*. Minneapolis: Augsburg, 1931.

Hamman, A. *Prayer: The New Testament*. Chicago: Franciscan Herald Press, 1971.

Häring, Bernard. *Prayer: The Integration of Faith and Life*. Notre Dame, Ind.: Fides Publishers, 1975.

Harkness, Georgia. *Prayer and the Common Life*. New York: Abingdon-Cokesbury Press, 1948.

Harner, Philip B. *Understanding the Lord's Prayer*. Philadelphia: Fortress, 1975.

Harper, Steve. *Prayer Ministry in the Local Church*. Grand Rapids: Baker, 1976.

Hassel, David J. *Radical Prayer*. New York: Paulist, 1983.

Hastings, James, ed. *The Great Christian Doctrines*. Edinburgh: T&T Clark, 1915.

Heiler, Friedrich. *Prayer: A Study in the History and Psychology of Religion*. New York: Oxford University Press, 1932.

Heschel, Abraham Joshua. *Quest for God*. New York: Crossroads, 1982.

Houston, James. *The Transforming Power of Prayer: Deepening Your Friendship with God*. Colorado Springs: NavPress, 1996.

Howe, Leroy T. *Prayer in a Secular World*. Philadelphia: United Church Press, 1973.

Humphreys, Fisher. *The Heart of Prayer*. Nashville: Broadman, 1980.

Hunter, W. Bingham. *The God Who Hears*. Downers Grove, Ill.: InterVarsity, 1986.

Ingle, George. *The Lord's Creed*. London: Collins Press, 1964.

Jennings, Theodore W. Jr. *Life as Worship: Prayer and Praise in Jesus' Name*. Grand Rapids: Eerdmans, 1982.

Johnson, Merle Allison. *Religious Roulette and Other Dangerous Games Christians Play*. Nashville: Abingdon, 1975.

Keller, W. Phillip. *A Layman Looks at the Lord's Prayer*. Minneapolis: World Wide Publications, 1976.

King, Geoffrey R. *Let Us Pray*. Fort Washington, Pa.: Christian Literature Crusade, n.d.

Knapp-Fisher, E. G. *Belief and Prayer*. London: Darton, Longman & Todd, 1964.

Koenig, John. *Rediscovering New Testament Prayer: Boldness and Blessing in the Name of Jesus*. San Francisco: Harper San Francisco, 1992.

Laubach, Frank. *Channels of Spiritual Power*. Westwood, N.J.: Revell, 1954.

Lavender, John Allan. *Why Prayers Are Unanswered*. Valley Forge, Pa.: Judson Press, 1967.

Laymon, Charles M. *The Lord's Prayer*. Nashville: Abingdon, 1968.

Leech, Kenneth. *True Prayer*. New York: Harper & Row, 1980.

LeFevre, Perry. *Radical Prayer: Contemporary Interpretations*. Chicago: Exploration Press, 1982.

————. *Understandings of Prayer*. Philadelphia: Westminster, 1981.

Lewis, C. S. *Letters to Malcolm: Chiefly on Prayer*. New York: Harcourt, Brace & World, 1963.

Lindsell, Harold. *When You Pray*. Wheaton, Ill.: Tyndale House, 1969.

Lockyer, Herbert. *All the Prayers of the Bible*. Grand Rapids: Zondervan, 1959.

Loew, Jacques. *Face to Face with God*. New York: Paulist, 1977.

Lohmeyer, Ernst. *"Our Father": An Introduction to the Lord's Prayer*. New York: Harper & Row, 1965.

Louf, Andre. *Teach Us to Pray*. New York: Paulist, 1975.

Luthi, Walter. *The Lord's Prayer*. Richmond, Va.: John Knox, 1961.

Maclachlan, Lewis. *Twenty-One Steps to Positive Prayer*. Valley Forge, Pa.: Judson Press, 1978.

Magee, John. *Reality and Prayer*. New York: Harper & Brothers, 1957.

May, Gerald G. *Pilgrimage Home: The Conduct of Contemplative Practice in Groups*. New York: Paulist, 1979.

Merton, Thomas. *Contemplative Prayer*. Garden City, N.Y.: Doubleday–Image Books, 1971.

Micks, Marianne H. *The Joy of Worship*. Philadelphia: Westminster, 1982.

Miller, Basil. *Prayer Meetings That Made History*. Anderson, Ind.: Warner Press, 1938.

Miskotte, Kornelis H. *The Roads of Prayer*. Translated by John W. Doberstein. New York: Sheed & Ward, 1968.

Mooney, Christopher F., ed. *Prayer: The Problem of Dialogue with God*. New York: Paulist, 1969.

Murphy, Miriam. *Prayer in Action*. Nashville: Abingdon, 1979.

Murray, Andrew. *The Ministry of Intercession*. New York: Revell, 1898.

————. *The Prayer-Life*. Garden City, N.Y.: Doubleday, Doran & Co., 1929.

————. *Waiting on God*. London: Oliphants, 1961.

———— *With Christ in the School of Prayer*. Old Tappan, N.J.: Revell, 1953.

Myers, Warren, and Ruth Myers. *Pray: How to Be Effective in Prayer*. Colorado Springs: NavPress, 1983.

Nedoncelle, Maurice. *The Nature and Use of Prayer*. London: Burns & Oates, 1964.

Nee, Watchman. *The Prayer Ministry of the Church*. New York: Christian Fellowship Publishers, 1973.

Northcott, Hubert. *Man, God, and Prayer*. London: SPCK, 1959.

————. *The Venture of Prayer*. London: SPCK, 1962.

Parker, William R., and Elaine St. Johns. *Prayer Can Change Your Life*. Englewood Cliffs, N.J.: Prentice Hall, 1957.

Parks, Helen Jean. *Holding the Ropes.* Nashville: Broadman, 1983.

Peterson, Eugene H. *Earth and Altar: The Community of Prayer in a Self-Bound Society.* Downers Grove, Ill.: InterVarsity, 1985.

Phelps, Austin. *The Still Hour.* Boston: D. Lothrop Company, 1893.

Phillips, D. Z. *The Concept of Prayer.* 1965; Oxford, U.K.: Basil Blackwell, 1981.

Pittenger, Norman. *Praying Today.* Grand Rapids: Eerdmans, 1974.

Powell, Cyril H. *Secrets of Answered Prayer.* New York: Thomas Y. Crowell, 1958.

Radcliffe, Lynn James. *Making Prayer Real.* New York: Abingdon-Cokesbury Press, 1952.

Rahner, Karl, S. J. *On Prayer.* New York: Paulist, 1968.

Reinberger, Francis E. *How to Pray.* Philadelphia: Fortress, 1964.

Rhea, Carolyn. *Come Pray with Me.* Grand Rapids: Zondervan, 1977.

Rhymes, Douglas. *Prayer in the Secular City.* Philadelphia: Westminster, 1967.

Rinker, Rosalind. *Prayer: Conversing with God.* Grand Rapids: Zondervan, 1959.

Saliers, Don E. *The Soul in Paraphrase.* New York: Seabury Press, 1980.

Sanders, J. Oswald. *Prayer Power Unlimited.* Minneapolis: World Wide Publications, 1977.

Saphir, Adolph. *The Hidden Life.* New York: Gospel Publishing House, n.d.

Scroggie, W. Graham. *Method in Prayer.* London: Pickering & Inglis, 1955.

Shoemaker, Helen Smith. *Power through Prayer Groups.* Westwood, N.J.: Revell, 1958.

Simpson, Robert L. *The Interpretation of Prayer in the Early Church.* Philadelphia: Westminster, 1965.

Stanley, David M. *Boasting in the Lord.* New York: Paulist, 1973.

———. *Jesus in Gethsemane.* New York: Paulist, 1980.

Steere, Douglas V. *Dimensions of Prayer.* New York: Harper & Row, 1962.

Strauss, Lehman. *Sense and Nonsense about Prayer.* Chicago: Moody, 1974.

Taylor, Jack R. *Prayer: Life's Limitless Reach.* Nashville: Broadman, 1977.

Thayer, Nelson, S.T. *Spirituality and Pastoral Care.* Philadelphia: Fortress, 1985.

Thomson, James, G. S. S. *The Praying Christ.* Grand Rapids: Eerdmans, 1959.

Torrey, R. A. *How to Pray.* Chicago: Moody, n.d.

———. *Power and Peace in Prayer.* Westchester, Ill.: Good News Publishers, n.d.

———. *The Power of Prayer.* Grand Rapids: Zondervan, 1955.

Ulanov, Ann, and Barry Ulanov. *Primary Speech: A Psychology of Prayer.* Atlanta: John Knox, 1982.

Vischer, Lukas. *Intercession.* Geneva: World Council of Churches, 1980.

Waddams, Herbert M. *Life and Fire of Love.* London: SPCK, 1964.

Ward, J. Neville. *The Use of Praying.* London: Epworth Press, 1967.

Whiston, Charles. *Pray: A Study of Distinctively Christian Prayer.* Grand Rapids: Eerdmans, 1972.

———. *Teach Us to Pray.* Boston: Pilgrim Press, 1949.

————. *When Ye Pray, Say Our Father.* Boston: Pilgrim Press, 1960.

Whyte, Alexander. *Lord, Teach Us to Pray.* New York: Doubleday, Doran & Co., n.d.

Williamson, Robert L. *Effective Public Prayer.* Nashville: Broadman, 1960.

Willis, Edward David. *Daring Prayer.* Atlanta: John Knox, 1977.

Winward, Stephen F. *Teach Yourself to Pray.* New York: Harper & Brothers, 1961.

Wright, John H. *A Theology of Christian Prayer.* New York: Pueblo Publishing Co., 1979.

Wuellner, Flora Slosson. *Prayer and the Living Christ.* Nashville: Abingdon, 1969.

Wyon, Olive. *The School of Prayer.* New York: Macmillan, 1963.

Essays about Prayer

Basinger, David. "Why Petition an Omnipotent, Omniscient, Wholly Good God?" *Religious Studies* 19, no. 1 (1983): 25-41.

Capps, Donald. "The Psychology of Petitionary Prayer." *Theology Today* 39, no. 2 (1982): 130-41.

Conn, Harvie M. "Luke's Theology of Prayer." *Christianity Today,* 22 December 1972, pp. 290-92.

Dalbey, Gordon. "Recovering Healing Prayer." *Christian Century,* 9 June 1982, pp. 690-93.

de Goedt, Michael. "The Intercession of the Spirit in Christian Prayer (Rom. 8:26-27)." In *The Prayer Life,* edited by Christian Duquoc and Claude Geffre, pp. 26-38. New York: Herder & Herder, 1972.

Goetz, Ronald. "Lord, Teach Us to Pray." *Christian Century,* 5 November 1986, pp. 974-76.

Hendry, George S. "The Life Line of Theology." *Princeton Seminary Bulletin* 65, no. 2 (1972): 22-30.

Huxhold, Harry N. "What Is the Place of Pastoral Prayer in the Context of Worship?" *Encounter* 43, no. 4 (1982): 395-400.

Ledogar, Robert. "Table Prayers and Eucharist: Questions from the Social Sciences." In *Prayer and Community,* edited by Herman Schmidt, pp. 104-16. New York: Herder & Herder, 1970.

Meninger, William. "Aspects of Prayer." In *Word and Spirit: A Monastic Review.* Still River, Mass.: St. Bede's Publications, 1982.

Mitchell, Curtis C. "The Case for Persistence in Prayer." *Journal of the Evangelical Theological Society* 27, no. 2 (1984): 161-68.

————. "Don't Pray for the Unsaved!" *Christianity Today,* 16 September 1983, pp. 28-29.

Owens, Virginia Stem. "Prayer — Into the Lion's Jaws." *Christianity Today,* 19 November 1976, pp. 17-21.

Patterson, LeRoy. "The Ten Most Unwanted Public Prayer Habits." *Eternity,* October 1982, pp. 35-36.

Wells, David F. "Prayer: Rebelling against the Status Quo." *Christianity Today,* 2 November 1979, pp. 32-34.

Other Books and Essays

Barclay, William. *Daily Bible Readings.* Glasgow: McCorquodale & Co., n.d.

————. *The Daily Study Bible.* Toronto: G. R. Welch Co., 1975.

James, William. *The Varieties of Religious Experience.* New York: New American Library, 1958.

Jones, E. Stanley. *The Way to Power and Poise.* New York: Abingdon-Cokesbury Press, 1959.

Kittel, Gerhard, and Gerhard Friedrich, eds. *Theological Dictionary of the New Testament.* Translated by Geoffrey W. Bromiley. 10 vols. Grand Rapids: Eerdmans, 1964.

Lewis, C. S. *God in the Dock.* Grand Rapids: Eerdmans, 1973.

Price, Robert M. "Illness Theodicies in the New Testament." *Journal of Religion and Health* 25, no. 4 (1986): 309-15.

Tennis, Diane. *Is God the Only Reliable Father?* Philadelphia: Westminster, 1985.

Trench, Richard C. *Synonyms of the New Testament.* Grand Rapids: Eerdmans, 1975.